Farewell to Alexandria

Farewell
to Alexandria

Solutions to space, growth, and performance problems of libraries

Edited by DANIEL GORE

GREENWOOD PRESS
WESTPORT, CONNECTICUT ● LONDON, ENGLAND

Library of Congress Cataloging in Publication Data

Main entry under title:

Farewell to Alexandria.

Includes bibliographical references and index.
1. Libraries—Addresses, essays, lectures. I. Gore, Daniel.
Z664.F27   021   75-35345
ISBN 0-8371-8587-4

Library of Congress Catalog Card Number: 75-35345
ISBN: 0-8371-8587-4

First published in 1976
Second printing 1977

Greenwood Press, Inc.
51 Riverside Avenue, Westport, Connecticut 06880

Printed in the United States of America

for john and meadows

Contents

Farewell to Alexandria

Introduction

The publication of this collection of essays opens a new era for libraries, taking the first departure in 2,300 years from that durable model conceived by the librarians of Alexandria and endlessly replicated by every succeeding generation of librarians, right down to the present day. The Alexandrian model persists through the unexamined faith that to be good a library *must* be vast and always growing. The papers presented here examine that faith scientifically, demonstrate that it rests on nothing more solid than mistaken intuition, and consign it to the limbo of outworn dogmas.

With capital funds for new library construction rapidly disappearing, this collective departure from the Alexandrian model could not have been better timed, for it can take us swiftly in the direction of improving real service to readers, while drastically slowing growth of collections or halting it altogether. Enormous outlays of capital funds for new library building construction, amounting to several billion dollars over the last ten years, did not solve the space problems of libraries. Indeed, among academic libraries it appears that the space problem was even a little worse at the end of the building boom than at its beginning.

If capital funding on the grand scale failed to solve the problem, then its sudden disappearance should not be so potent a cause for despair as is popularly imagined. Intellectual capital can more than compensate for diminution of the other kind, and between these covers you will find it in sufficient abundance to turn your present adversity into bright opportunity, if you have the vision and the will to reach for it.

All of the contributions to this volume, except the last, were presented at a conference sponsored by The Associated Colleges of the Midwest, held in Chicago, April 17-18, 1975. Entitled "Touching Bottom in the Bottomless Pit," the conference was intended to open a national debate on space, growth, and performance problems of libraries—academic libraries in particular, but other types as well. Some 230 librarians participated in the conference, coming from all quarters of the nation, with a sizable representation from Canada.

Issues of great magnitude are not settled in a two-day conference: they are opened and explored, argued and reflected upon. What was remarkable and prophetic about this conference was the willingness, nay the *eagerness*, of so many librarians, all of them holding positions of significant responsibility in the nation's libraries, to entertain seriously that most heretical of questions: Can library growth be curbed or halted without detriment to the central mission of librarians, namely the provision of books to readers? Of those in attendance, many insisted that such a troubling question can be answered affirmatively and that the answer can be converted into effective action—if not immediately, then certainly in the foreseeable future. But before there can be any effective action, on the scale needed to resolve our present space and performance crisis, there must first be a period of intense and searching thought, of careful and widespread investigation, leading to the formation of widely shared convictions upon which group action can be fruitfully founded. This volume marks the opening of that period.

Good wine needs no bush. The contributors to this collection are all seasoned professionals, most of them well known for their published work, the others destined to be so. Their work needs no flattery from an editor to commend it to your attention. It is fully capable of standing on its own merits and is presented here essentially as it came into the editor's hands, with only occasional, and slight, editorial intervention when it appeared possible to add a little polish to the general clarity of the original.

The keenest pleasure in forming such a volume comes in acknowledging the gracious help of the people who made it possible. The most obvious debt is to those who spoke at the conference and offered their papers for publication. Their names appear on the conference program, reproduced at the end of the volume. To Dan Martin, president of The Associated Colleges of the Midwest, I wish to express again my deep appreciation for his lively and constructive interest in the conference's venturesome theme, his generous offer to sponsor the conference under the aegis of The Associated Colleges of the Midwest, and his brisk and able performance as moderator of the panel discussion, printed here as a particularly vocal and provocative ornament to the collection. Jeanette McGrath of the ACM staff handled all the complex conference arrangements with such alacrity, meticulousness, and good-natured ease, she left me and all the conferees with the agreeable illusion that it was simply not *possible* for anything to go wrong. Nothing did, and that speaks volumes—to which I add here an equal measure of praise and thanks for that incomparable result. Judith Anne Duncan, calligrapher to the Macalester College Library, did the splendid calligraphic and other spritely art work for the conference brochure and program, which added a special pleasure (both literal and visual) to the proceedings.

Finally I want to thank my secretary Mrs. Dorothy Barnes for preparing the manuscript of this volume for publication and for overseeing the elaborate promotional work that led to such a fine turnout for the conference. Taking on those tasks in addition to her usual extensive library assignments constitutes, in my eyes, an authentic miracle—something I have learned over the years I can routinely count on her to create whenever the occasion requires it. That is a very good feeling to have, as is the gratitude it continually inspires among all of us who work with her.

D.G.
Macalester College
St. Paul, Minnesota
June 10, 1975

Claudia Schorrig

Sizing Up the Space Problem in Academic Libraries

Most libraries now have a space problem to solve, or soon will. Historically, libraries have exhausted book storage space long before they were designed to. I will not dwell on the reasons for this problem here, but the general causes are clear: volume of publication has reached astronomic proportions and shows no sign of receding; the librarian's urge to keep pace with that volume, combined with a reluctance to weed heavily, has led inevitably to prematurely overloaded libraries.

During the biggest building boom in library history, 1967 to 1974, book collections grew a little faster than the new space to hold them. Hence, when the boom was over, the aggregate space problem was just a little worse than it was at the beginning.

During the roughly eight-year span of the boom, about 570 new or expanded library buildings were built on the campuses of four-year and graduate institutions throughout this nation. It was, in the words of Jerrold Orne, "the greatest flowering of academic library building experience this country has ever known or is likely to see."[1] This flowering generated new building space to accommodate 163 million additional volumes. But aggregate collection growth over the same time span added up to 166 million volumes: three million more than space was provided for. (See Appendix I for data sources and analysis that yield these results.) This space deficit would have been fivefold worse except for the weeding of 12 million volumes from academic library collections during the boom years. Had the weeding not taken place concurrently with the building, the failure of efforts to solve the space problem by adding more space would have been perceived sooner.

It seems evident that, even in the most affluent times, our efforts to solve geometric growth architecturally are undermined by our accelerated acquisitions. Obviously, libraries cannot keep up with the book publishers, although, as my surveys indicate, they have tried.

What happened to academic libraries in 1973 and 1974 may be understood as prologue to the mounting space problems that lie ahead. In those two waning years of the building boom, total shelving capacity increased by only 25 million volumes, while net collection growth came to 41 million. Space deficits cumulating at the rate of 8 million volumes per year point to widespread crisis conditions that are close at hand, or already beset us.

Although the slightly negative outcome of the great building boom is sufficiently disconcerting as an aggregate result, it is important to note that the distribution of all that new building capacity is quite lopsided. For though some 570 campuses acquired new building space during the boom, a thousand other campuses did not.[2] Now the 166 million volumes that were added during the boom years clearly did not land exclusively on the shelves of those 570 libraries that added *all* of the new building capacity. Millions of new books streamed into the thousand libraries that did not add shelving capacity during those years. Since all those libraries are today at least nine years old, and most of them older than that, and since most academic libraries doubled their holdings over the last ten years, the dimension of the space problem in those thousand libraries that missed the building boom has surely reached crisis proportions. But their plight calls more for remedy than proof; hence, I have given most of my attention in the following survey to a selected group of those libraries whose shelving capacity *was* expanded in the boom years.

Individual Survey

To estimate the magnitude of the space problem today for those libraries that shared in the building boom,[3] and what it is likely to be in a decade, I sent a questionnaire to all 272 libraries that acquired a new building or an addition in 1967 and 1968. (See Appendix II for an example of the questionnaire sent.) Of this group, 89 libraries—about one out of three—returned the questionnaire (Appendix III). Perhaps the others were too busy shifting collections and weeding to make their plight known. Henceforth, I shall speak only of these 89 libraries when reporting frequency count, percentages, maximum capacity, volumes bought, and so on.

Two assumptions are made in this analysis: (1) that the projections reported by libraries are accurate, and (2) that the number of volumes added between 1974 and 1984 remains constant in each consecutive year. My intent is to get trend indications rather than scientific accuracy. But even allowing for error, the figures are mind-boggling.

Volumes held in 1964 totaled 19,473,594 (Table 1). The addition of 18,487,826 volumes between 1964 and 1974 brings the total to 37,961,420. This total represents 73.6 percent of *absolute maximum shelf capacity* for these institutions, which comes to 51,545,659. The number of volumes estimated to be held in 1984 is 59,842,623, an increase of 21,881,203 volumes from 1974; that will bring the aggregate load factor to 116.09 percent of the aggregate maximum capacity of 51,545,659 volumes. Between 1964 and 1984, a total of 40,369,029 volumes will have been added. In short, total volumes held by the 89 libraries in 1964 was 19.5 million. By 1974 collections had nearly doubled in size, reaching 38 million volumes. By 1984, collections are expected to grow to 59.8 million.

The shelf load factor of these 89 relatively new libraries is surprisingly high (Table 2). Let's pause here a moment to define terms. *Maximum efficient shelf capacity* is commonly construed to be around 75 percent of *absolute* maximum. Put another way, when every 36-inch shelf in your stacks carries 27 linear inches of books, then your stacks are 75 percent loaded, but they have nonetheless reached maximum *efficient* capacity. Loading beyond that level (in a classified collection) requires so much internal shifting to accommodate new books that it is generally believed more economical to construct new stack capacity than to utilize more than 75 percent of what is already available. In 1974 the 89 libraries responding to the survey, though only about seven years old, had already reached an *average* of 74 percent maximum absolute capacity. By 1980 they will be at the 100 percent level, in the aggregate.

Analytical results naturally present some startling constrasts with the average picture of the group. In 1974, 35 of the libraries, or 40 percent of the sample, had already reached maximum efficient shelf load or exceeded it. Two libraries had even passed *absolute* maximum capacity at this point, only six or seven years after they were built.

By 1977, a total of 51 libraries (57.3 percent) will have reached 75 percent or greater shelf loads; and 24 (27 percent) libraries will have shelf loads over 100 percent maximum capacity.

TABLE 1. Volumes Held (*Frequency Count*)

Volumes (In thousands)	1964	1974 Including Storages & Branches	1984 Projected Volumes	Maximum Capacity (100%)
0-050	22	3	0	3
51-100	28	22	10	5
101-150	9	12	15	14
151-200	6	12	12	14
201-250	2	4	4	6
251-300	3	3	5	9
301-350	2	5	1	5
351-400	0	1	6	1
401-450	1	6	2	1
451-500	1	2	1	4
501-550	0	0	3	2
551-600	0	1	0	1
601-650	0	1	1	1
651-700	2	0	3	2
701-750	1	0·	2	1
751-800	2	0	1	0
801-850	0	1	1	0
851-900	1	3	1	1
901-950	0	0	0	0
951-1,000	0	1	2	4
1,001-1,050	1	1	0	0
1,051-1,100	0	2	1	2
1,101-1,150	1	1	0	0
1,151-1,200	1	1	0	2
1,201-1,250	0	0	0	1
1,251-1,300	0	1	0	
1,301-1,350	0	1	1	
1,351-1,400	0	0	0	1
1,401-1,450	0	0	0	
1,451-1,500	0	0	1	1
1,501-1,550	0	0	1	
1,551-1,600	0	1	1	2
1,601-1,650	0	0	0	
1,651-1,700	0	1	0	
1,701-1,750	0	1	2	1
1,751-1,800	0	0	0	
1,801-1,850	0	0	1	
1,851-1,900	0	0	0	
1,901-1,950	0	0	0	1
1,951-2,000	0	0	2	
2,001-2,500	1	0	3	2
2,501-3,000	0	1	1	
3,001-3,500	0	0	1	
3,501-4,000	0	1	1	
4,001-4,500	0	0	0	1
4,501-5,000	0	0	0	
5,001-5,500	0	0	1	1
Total	84	89	86	89
Missing Data	5		3	

AGGREGATE DATA

Total Volumes held in 1964:   19,473,594

Total Volumes held in 1974:   37,961,420   Increase in Volumes = 18,487,826
                                            73.6% of Total Capacity Loaded

Projected Volumes in 1984:   59,842,623   Increase in Volumes = 21,881,203
                                            116.09% Loaded

MAXIMUM CAPACITY TOTAL = 51,545,659

TOTAL VOLUMES BOUGHT 1964-84:   40,369,029

TABLE 2. Shelf Load Factor (100% Maximum Capacity)

A.

Percent Loaded	1974		1977		1984	
	Frequency Count	Percent	Frequency Count	Percent	Frequency Count	Percent
0-20	1	1.1	1	1.1	1	1.1
21-40	4	4.5	1	1.1	0	0.0
41-60	22	24.7	16	18.0	4	4.5
61-80	38	42.7	32	36.0	17	19.1
81-100	22	24.7	15	17.0	22	24.7
over 100	2	2.2	24	27.0	45	50.5
Total	89		89		89	

B. Synopsis

Percent Loaded	1974		1977		1984	
	Frequency Count	Percent	Frequency Count	Percent	Frequency Count	Percent
75% or Greater	35	39.3	51	57.3	75	84.3
81%-100% or Greater	24	26.9	39	44.0	67	75.3
81%-86%*	10	11.0	8	9.0	8	9.0
Greater than 100%	2	22.2	24	27.0	45	50.5

*"Complete Working Capacity", according to Keyes Metcalf: Planning Academic and Research Library Buildings (New York: McGraw-Hill, 1965), p. 155.

In 1984, a decade from now (using the projected number of volumes anticipated by each library), 75 institutions (84.3 percent) will be 75 percent or greater loaded; and 45 (50.5 percent) will have shelf loads over 100 percent maximum capacity.

While it is unclear just how each library computed its shelving capacity and if future additional shelving was figured in, the survey leaves no doubt that, as a group, they are running out of space. Although the data indicate some anticipated decline in growth rates during the ten years ahead, the average lifespan, or capacity, of these relatively new libraries works out to about thirteen years.

When considering the options that might be exercised when maximum efficient book capacity is reached (see Table 3), not one library opted for placing volumes in a branch library; 9 (10.1 percent) would build a new library; 40 (44.9 percent) would add to the existing library; only 25 (28.1 percent) would install compact shelving; 24 (27

TABLE 3. Options That Will Be Exercised at the Main Library When Maximum Efficient Capacity Is Reached

			Frequency Count	Percentage
1.	Place in Branch Library	Yes	0	
		No	89	100.0
2.	Build New Library	Yes	9	10.1
		No	80	89.9
3.	Add to Existing Library	Yes	40	44.9
		No	49	55.1
4.	Install Compact Shelving	Yes	25	28.1
		No	64	71.9
5.	Develop Separate Storage Facility	Yes	24	27.0
		No	65	73.0
6.	Convert Journal runs to Microfilm	Yes	47	52.8
		No	42	47.2
7.	Other Solutions	Yes	22	24.7
		No	67	75.3

percent) would develop a separate storage facility; but 47 (52.8 percent) would convert journal runs to microfilm. "Other solutions" ranged from "Handwringing" to "Punt!" The most often cited were the conversion of reader stations to shelving space, addition of shelving, and transfer to storage facility (even if presently nonexistent). Other solutions proposed were to weed extensively, develop cooperative arrangements with nearby universities for storage, weed and microfilm, remodel, maximize purchase of microforms, store journals in cooperative facility, convert display and browsing areas to shelf space and develop a zero growth rate by extensive weeding to provide room for new acquisitions. Multipurpose buildings are also utilizing classrooms as a spillover. Several libraries were planned with built-in options to expand vertically by adding another floor, or to make use of space now occupied by other departments. One library plans to stay at its 160,000-volume level for a period of time through larger withdrawals. Finally, one college is hoping that this conference will help them to plan.

Only 22 libraries of the 89 (24.7 percent) presently have a storage facility (Table 4); the aggregate capacity is 2.5 million volumes. The aggregate present content of these storage facilities is 1.9 million volumes (Table 5), which means that 77.3 percent of all storage is already loaded.

TABLE 4

LIBRARIES PRESENTLY HAVING A STORAGE FACILITY

Yes	%	No	%
22	24.7	67	75.3

ABSOLUTE MAXIMUM CAPACITY OF STORAGE FACILITY

VOLUMES	FREQUENCY COUNT	RELATIVE PERCENT
400	1	1.1
1,000	1	1.1
5,400	1	1.1
9,387	1	1.1
10,000	2	2.2
20,000	1	1.1
22,808	1	1.1
24,990	1	1.1
25,000	2	2.2
35,000	1	1.1
58,000	1	1.1
70,000	2	2.2
80,000	2	2.2
81,648	1	1.1
100,000	1	1.1
234,000	1	1.1
243,900	1	1.1
1,500,000	1	1.1
Total Storage Capacity 2,521,533	22	

In selecting volumes for transfer to storage, most libraries utilized at least three of the criteria listed in the questionnaire (Table 6). Most often chosen were the following, in descending order: date of publication, judgment of a subject specialist, frequency of recorded use, language of text, and last recorded circulation date. (Dr. Trueswell, I believe, will have a good deal to say about the last-named criterion later in this conference.)

Conclusion

The 89 libraries responding to the survey reported that their collections had grown nearly 95 percent between 1964 and 1974, from 19.5 to 38.0 million volumes. By 1984 they anticipate that their col-

TABLE 5. *Storage Facility's Present Content*

VOLUMES	FREQUENCY COUNT	RELATIVE PERCENT
0	1	1. 1
90	1	1. 1
175	1	1. 1
2, 000	1	1. 1
3, 000	2	2. 2
5, 000	3	3. 4
12, 495	1	1. 1
14, 593	1	1. 1
20, 000	1	1. 1
25, 000	3	3. 4
50, 000	1	1. 1
58, 000	1	1. 1
60, 000	1	1. 1
70, 000	1	1. 1
180, 000	1	1. 1
675, 000	1	1. 1
774, 525	1	1. 1

Total Present
Storage
Content   1, 949, 878   22

Summary: Total Maximum Capacity of All Storage   2, 521, 533
                Total Present Content of Storage   1, 949, 878

                Percent of Total Storage Loaded: 77. 3

lections will grow to 59.8 million volumes, an increase of only 58 percent over the next decade, as compared with a 95 percent-rate of increase in the previous decade. This represents a steep and significant decline in the anticipated growth rate. But while the rate of growth is expected to decline, the number of volumes actually added each year is expected to increase. If the data from these 89 libraries typify the national situation, then aggregate growth over the next eight years will be at the rate of 22 million volumes per year. Yet, during the eight years of the building boom, aggregate growth was just 20 million volumes per year.

TABLE 6.   Criteria Used in Selecting Volumes for Transfer to Storage (22 Libraries Presently Having Storage Facility)

			Frequency Count	Percentage
1.	Last Recorded Circulation Date	Yes	8	36.4
		No	14	63.6
2.	Frequency of Recorded Use	Yes	11	50
		No	11	50
3.	Date of Publication	Yes	14	63.6
		No	8	36.4
4.	Language of Text	Yes	9	40.9
		No	13	59.1
5.	Judgement of Specialist	Yes	12	54.5
		No	10	45.5
6.	Other Criteria	Yes	6	27.3
		No	16	72.7

Only a staunch remnant of optimists would anticipate a building boom over the next eight years to equal or exceed that of the last eight, when all economic indicators are pointing the other way.

We are faced with two conflicting anticipations. On the one hand, we expect collection growth to increase, and, on the other, we expect building growth to decline. How then will we deal with the rapidly mounting excess of books over shelving that is bound to ensue?

Notes

1. Jerrold Orne, "The Renaissance of Academic Library Building, 1967-71," *Library Journal*, (December 1, 1971): 3947. In the passage quoted, Dr. Orne refers to the five-year period 1967-1971.
2. I note here that two-year institutions have been omitted from consideration in this survey only because the necessary building data are unavailable. But one may reasonably assume that their situation does not differ greatly from the others.
3. Orne, pp. 3953-3967. Survey libraries were selected from this list.

APPENDIX I:
Analysis of Aggregate Building and Collection-Growth Data

SHELVING CAPACITY ADDED, 1967-1974

Data here are taken from Jerrold Orne's series of American academic library building reports, which appear in each December 1 issue of

Library Journal, and cover (with the exception of the five-year cumu-
lation noted below) building completions of the calendar year in
which the report appears. Orne excludes two-year college libraries
from his report, but includes Canadian senior institutions.

According to Orne (*LJ*, December 1, 1971, p. 3947), the total shelving capacity added in the five-year period 1967-1971 was 127,377,821
volumes. This figure also includes Canadian libraries, whose added
capacity must thus be subtracted to obtain a figure for U.S. academic
libraries. Adding Orne's individual listings for Canadian libraries on
p. 3967 of the same *LJ* issue, I get a rounded total of 8,929,000 volumes added shelf capacity. Subtracting this sum from Orne's grand
total, and rounding the result, gives us 118,449,000 volumes new
capacity in American academic libraries (excluding two-year institutions) for the period 1967-1971. I obtained data for subsequent years
simply by adding all the listings in Orne's reports and in all categories
except Canadian libraries. I count a renovation project as new
capacity, except where Orne has made a specific distinction between
new and renovated capacity in connection with a renovation project.
Any error of interpretation here would have the effect of making new
building capacity appear somewhat larger than it actually was.

COMPLETION DATE OF BUILDING	CAPACITY ADDED	NO. OF BLDGS.
1967-1971	118,449,000 vols.	445
1972	15,770,000	36
1973	8,979,000	29
Built but not reported prior to 1973	1,396,000	6
1974	15,805,000	52
Built but not reported prior to 1974	1,704,000	4
TOTALS:	162,103,000 vols.	572

VOLUMES ADDED TO COLLECTIONS, 1967-1974

Data for this section come from *The Bowker Annual of Library &
Book Trade Information*, 19th edition, 1974, p. 258. There is a
difficulty here, because these summary data for college and university
libraries include data for two-year colleges, lumping all into one category. But Orne's building data exclude two-year colleges, so to make
the data comparable one must either discover building data for
two-year colleges (which I believe is not obtainable for the period in
question) or find some means to segregate collection data of two-year
colleges from the total. There is little in the literature to help here. But

Theodore Samore, a recognized authority on academic library statistics, calculates that for the period in question the acquisitions of two-year college libraries represent 10 percent of the reported total. (Personal communication from Mr. Samore to Mr. Daniel Gore.)

To arrive at a net growth figure for any given period, one must also take into account the number of volumes withdrawn. A complete sample of the "Volumes Withdrawn" columns on four pages taken at random from the Fall 1969 *Library Statistics of Colleges and Universities: Data for Individual Institutions* shows that volumes withdrawn came to 7 percent of those added. Data reported in the *Bowker Annual* ("Volumes at end of year" and "Volumes added during year") also provide a basis for calculating withdrawal rates, but gross anomalies in those correlations make that approach useless. So in the calculations below I have used the 7 percent withdrawal rate figure developed from individual library reports.

Aggregate data from the 78 ARL university libraries over a nine-year period yield approximately the same withdrawal rate. Data are taken from *Academic Library Statistics, 1963/64 to 1971/72. . .* (ERIC ED 082 791; Washington, ARL, 1972) and are as follows:

YEAR	VOLS. ADDED (GROSS)	VOLS. ADDED (NET)
1971/72	7,847,305	7,169,308
70/71	7,989,803	7,484,446
69/70	7,969,505	7,474,590
68/69	7,691,036	7,238,611
67/68	7,141,718	6,727,224
66/67	6,451,956	6,043,102
65/66	5,117,388	4,772,504
64/65	4,861,678	4,480,864
63/64	4,284,850	3,613,049
	59,355,239 vols.	55,003,698 vols.

The difference between gross and net indicates a withdrawal of 4,351,541 volumes over the nine-year period, or 7.3 percent of the total added.

For volumes added during 1974, I have used the estimated figure of 24 million, since the Bowker data only go through 1973. That estimate is one million less than the figure reported for 1973.

CALCULATIONS

Volumes added, 1967-1973 (from *Bowker Annual*)	174,000,000
Volumes added, 1974 (estimate)	24,000,000
Total:	198,000,000
Less 10% (estimated intake of two-year colleges)	19,800,000
Volumes added, 1967-1974, to four-year colleges & universities	178,200,000
Volumes withdrawn, 1967-1974, from four-year colleges & universities (based on 7% of intake)	12,400,000
NET ADDITION TO COLLECTIONS	165,800,000 vols.
NET ADDITION TO BUILDING CAPACITY	162,103,000 vols.
Space Deficit Created During Boom Years:	3,697,000 vols.

APPENDIX II:

Questionnaire – Survey of Academic Library Shelving Capacity

1. Name of library _____ City _____ State _____

2. Number of vols. in total collections   _____ vols.
   (including all branches and storage facilities)

3. Number of vols. in 1964   _____ vols.

4. Estimated number of vols. in 1984   _____ vols.

5. Absolute maximum capacity (in vols.) of the library   _____ vols.
   (including all branches and storage facilities, and
   assuming every shelf is 100% loaded)

6. Present shelf load factor   ____ %
   (Vols. held divided by absolute maximum capacity)

7. In what year was the main library (or its latest addition) occupied?   _____

8. In what year will the main library reach maximum *efficient* book capacity?
   (Generally reckoned at 75% of absolute maximum capacity)   _____

9. What options will you exercise at that time at the main library?
   (check all that fit)
       ( ) Place in Branch Library
       ( ) Build a new library
       ( ) Add to the existing library
       ( ) Install compact shelving
       ( ) Develop separate storage facility
       ( ) Convert journal runs to microfilm
       ( ) Other. Please specify: _____

10. Do you presently have a storage facility? Yes_____ No _____

11. If yes, what is the absolute maximum capacity of storage facility? _____ vols.

12. What is the storage facility's present content? _____ vols.

13. What criteria are used in selecting volumes for transfer to storage?
   (check all that fit)
       ( ) Last recorded circulation date
       ( ) Frequency of recorded use
       ( ) Date of publication
       ( ) Language of text
       ( ) Judgment of a subject specialist
       ( ) Other. Please specify: _____

10/17/74

APPENDIX III:
Academic Libraries That Responded to the Survey

Augustana College
Rock Island, Ill.

Eastern Illinois University
Charleston, Ill.

East Carolina University
Greenville, N.C.

Florida State University
Tallahassee, Fla.

Georgia College
Milledgeville, Ga.

Georgia State University
Atlanta, Ga.

Hartwick College
Oneonta, N.Y.

Haverford College
Haverford, Pa.

Loyola University
Chicago, Ill.

Maryville College
 of the Sacred Heart
St. Louis, Mo.

Michigan State University
East Lansing, Mich.

Oklahoma State University
Stillwater, Okla.

Randolph-Macon Woman's College
Lynchburg, Va.

Texas A & M University
College Station, Tex.

Texas Southern University
Houston, Tex.

University of California
Davis, Calif.

University of California
Santa Barbara, Calif.

University of Houston
Houston, Tex.

University of Minnesota
Duluth, Minn.

University of Southern California
Los Angeles, Calif.

University of Texas
El Paso, Tex.

University of Tulsa
Tulsa, Okla.

Western Michigan Univ.
Kalamazoo, Mich.

Ohio Northern University
Ada, Ohio

Pacific Lutheran University
Tacoma, Wash.

Pembroke State University
Pembroke, N.C.

Pfeiffer College
Misenheimer, N.C.

Portland State University
Portland, Oreg.

Providence College
Providence, R.I.

Quincy College
Quincy, Ill.

Rockhurst College
Kansas City, Mo.

St. Mary's College of California
Morage, Calif.

St. Mary's Dominican College
New Orleans, La.

St. Peter's College
Jersey City, N.J.

Shaw University
Raleigh, N.C.

Shippensburg State College
Shippensburg, Pa.

Southwest Texas State University
San Marcos, Tex.

Southwest Minnesota
State College
Marshall, Minn.

Southwestern State College
Weatherford, Okla.

Spalding College
Louisville, Ky.

State University of New York
College of Forestry at
Syracuse University
Syracuse, N.Y.

Texas A & I University
Kingsville, Tex.

Tulane University
New Orleans, La.

Agriculture, Mechanical &
Normal College
Pine Bluff, Ark.

Alabama Agricultural &
Mechanical University
Normal, Ala.

Austin Peay State University
Clarksville, Tenn.

Bemidji State College
Bemidji, Minn.

California State Polytechnic
College
Pomona, Calif.

College of the Southwest
Hobbs, N.M.

College of the Virgin Islands
St. Thomas, V.I.

De Anza College Learning
    Center
Cupertino, Calif.

Delta State College
Cleveland, Miss.

Eastern Michigan University
Ypsilanti, Mich.

Elon College
Elon College, N.C.

Emory & Henry College
Emory, Va.

Fairfield University
Fairfield, Conn.

Ferris State College
Big Rapids, Mich.

Findlay College
Findlay, Ohio

University of Florida
Gainesville, Fla.

University of Minnesota
Minneapolis, Minn.

University of Missouri
Rolla, Mo.

University of Montevallo
Montevallo, Ala.

University of Pittsburgh
Pittsburgh, Pa.

University of West Florida
Pensacola, Fla.

University of Wisconsin
Milwaukee, Wis.

Stanford University
Stanford, Calif.

University of Utah
Salt Lake City, Utah

Urbana College
Urbana, Ohio

Wisconsin State University
Platteville, Wis.

West Georgia College
Carrollton, Ga.

University of Hawaii
Honolulu, Hawaii

Southern Oregon College
Ashland, Oreg.

Louisiana State University
Alexandria, La.

Sacred Heart University
Bridgeport, Conn.

Florida Southern College
Lakeland, Fla.

Fontbonne College
St. Louis, Mo.

Graceland College
Lamoni, Iowa

Illinois Wesleyan University
Bloomington, Ill.

Heidelberg College
Tiffin, Ohio

Louisiana State University
Shreveport, La.

Lycoming College
Williamsport, Pa.

Mankato State College
Mankato, Minn.

Mary Baldwin College
Staunton, Va.

Marylhurst College
Marylhurst, Oreg.

Marymount College
Tarrytown, N.Y.

Memphis State University
Memphis, Tenn.

Milton College
Milton, Wis.

Nazareth College
Kalamazoo, Mich.

New England College
Henniker, N.H.

Ellsworth Mason

Balbus; or the Future of Library Buildings

If you collected the works of Robert Graves, as I do, you would have to be acquainted with the Today and Tomorrow series of books, published in the mid- and late 1920s by Kegan Paul, Trench, Trubner in London and by Dutton in New York. This series numbered more than a hundred rather brilliant, short monographs, on topics of social interest (which happily in those days were not swabbed with the cliché "controversial"). They purported to delineate the future, and their sales were enormously successful. Each title began with a Latin proper name, and Robert Graves's *Lars Porsena; or The Future of Swearing* went through six editions in four years. None of these books, of course, delineated the future with any accuracy at all, but even today most of them make very sprightly reading. With the title of my address, I therefore presume to join this great English tradition of highly literate, dynamically rationalized inaccuracy. However, I am not daunted by the thought that some of what I say may possibly turn out to be right.

The first approach to my task is to proceed entirely unencumbered by facts. Frequently this is the only approach taken to library problems, but as the day wears on I will supplement it with other approaches.

1. Let's expand the tiresome cliché "the right book to the right person at the right time" to read "the right *library* to the right person at the right time." The proper construct to answer this need is the variable-pitch space satellite library, which descends to the user at the press of a button and pours from a cornucopia the very books that he

needs. Now, I don't want to present this as a total answer, but if we can agree in this gathering that it is basically right in principle, we can apply for a feasibility grant and we are on our way.

2. For our next attempt we might try a fluid construct, to wit, energy, by adapting an idea of a highly erratic Yugoslav scientific genius named Nikola Tesla. Tesla spent some time in Colorado Springs, about forty years before I lived there, experimenting with ways to supercharge the electrical potential of the earth, by forcing more electricity into the ground than it could comfortably hold. Thus, you could tap electricity anywhere on earth by inserting a simple probe into the ground. There are still people living who believe that Tesla actually succeeded in his search, only to be bought out by General Electric. Be that as it may, why should not the same principle apply to leaves of printed matter, which could (and probably will) be jammed into the Library of Congress in such potential that they could be peeled out one by one at will in any public library in the nation?

3. Let's try a *square* approach. There is a multiple-breakthrough in the immediate future, although not yet operational, in the form of a new invention. It comes in His, Her, It, and Omnisex models. It is multichromatic-chameleon, assuming at once the color of its user. It is so cheap that as a universal blessing it will obviously be given away. It solves all problems of libraries by the simple process of bypassing them completely. It even bypasses the human mind, which is still the greatest known barrier to learning. This is a portable teaching machine, a cube measuring one inch square on each side, that imparts knowledge by means of electronically induced sphinctral vibrations.

This ends the innovative part of my presentation, and those who have come for innovation (that meaningless word), at a time in history when everything possible in human interaction has already been done a hundred times before, should leave, since what I say from now on threatens to have a certain amount of substance.

We have recently ground to a halt one of the most remarkable outbursts of building known to man. During 1967-1971, we built one billion dollars worth of academic library buildings alone. In this same period public library buildings and branch libraries multiplied all over the globe, the high school library became a reality, and the elementary school library began to rise. The money this nation poured into library buildings over this five-year period may have been as much as three billion dollars. This was about the net worth of the entire Roman Empire during the Augustan Age.

Since this period was fatuous in the extreme, the amount of money wasted on these buildings was astronomical. Older buildings that were easily expandable and convertible to new uses were razed in favor of plastic-fronted, glass-walled cages that now confront the energy shortage very uneasily. New buildings were built from depths of ignorance about library matters that made them useless. I have consulted on a library building to replace a new library building only four years old. Buildings called innovative utilized shapes such as circles, triangles, diamonds, stars, and hexagons that were perfectly serviceable to primitive man but were of dubious value or destructive to libraries. And since there are few limitations on cliches that have reached their time, with the infinite imagination that distinguishes morons we built libraries shaped like onions, cabbages, and dragonflies. Not to mention those great monuments to beauty in the American grocery-carton style throughout the land.

We larded these buildings with internal fountains, hanging gardens, mirrored walls, and other distractions beyond belief. I once confronted a board of trustees on the shores of Long Island bent on having a swimming pool on the roof and a boathouse in the basement of their library.

Now, I don't want to give you the impression that we were totally self-indulgent during this period. Nothing even in Texas, for instance, was shaped like a ten-gallon hat; no one floated carrels on gondolas in those internal fountains; and, although I have now been through more than five hundred library buildings, to the best of my knowledge none of the reading areas was equipped with rifle ranges or bowling alleys. If they had been, the lighting would undoubtedly have been planned better.

There were positive gains during this period. Most of the good small liberal arts colleges, long pressed to the wall in their library buildings, gathered their energies and built new buildings, many of them good. Colorado College, for instance, replaced in 1962 a library built in 1894. A few of the great horrors, such as the old University of Chicago Library, which was bad the day it opened, were replaced with highly successful buildings. Most libraries built during this period observed the principles of modular construction. We began to understand to some degree the importance of lighting, of the feeling of the interior design, and of comfortable temperatures in generating use of the library. Above all, we learned the importance of writing a building program before planning the building.

Right now, I think that we are about to be driven, through want, into the condition that has to precede the writing of any successful building program—a sophisticated understanding of what we want to accomplish in the building in response to sensitively understood needs of the users that emerge from the academic program. In recent years a range of people in different disciplines, with different interests, have begun to study exactly what happens to the movements of people and of books in the use of libraries. As a result of this information, the kind of information that was in the heads of good sixteenth-century librarians, we are revising our conceptions of all kinds of things and abandoning all kinds of fictions.

For instance, although not in all cases proved for the ages, the following recent information about academic dynamics seems to be true:

1. Students who do not check books out of the library still are, to a considerable extent, serious and steady users of the library and its collections. When we analyzed our circulation records and identified those students at the University of Colorado who had not charged out one book during the previous year and interviewed them, a large number turned out to be users of the library and of library books, some of them daily users.

2. Many disciplines, or parts of disciplines, can work very successfully at levels right up through advanced research without much use of the library. In recruiting over a period of a year and a half, with the help of our Sociology Department, for a combined reference-sociology librarian, it became clear that of the twenty or so separate specialties now loosely covered by the label "sociology," very few depended on the library for teaching, research teaching, or research. To answer the question that springs immediately to your minds, our department is highly regarded by its peers in other universities.

Very advanced research of a highly specialized nature is completely independent of the library. In highly specialized, and especially in highly technical, research fields, the four or five practitioners of the specialty anticipate publication of results far in advance by communications among themselves.

3. Science and technology generate far greater use of university library collections than the humanities or social sciences. In an analysis of circulation by title at Ohio State University, which arranges titles in descending order of use, you have to plow through at least a third of the list before encountering even one humanities or social science title. The local nonscientists explain this fact by claiming far greater

on-premise use of library materials. However, follow-up casual obser-
vation in that library system indicates that the science libraries get at
least as much on-premise use as the nonscience libraries.

4. The books and periodicals which librarians and faculty consider
to be highly important often turn out to be very little used. After a review of the solidity of our periodicals list at Hofstra University, we
counted the use by titles over the next two years and found as many as
30 percent of them unused in some subject fields, much to the be-
wilderment of the faculty and ourselves.

5. Greatly increased access to information about the location of a
greatly increased range of library materials does not increase the
volume of interlibrary loans. Afer three years of participation in the
Ohio College Library Center (OCLC), the volume of interlibrary loans
among Ohio academic libraries has not increased.

6. Publications of the past ten years do not account for the overwhelming use of books. Analysis of interlibrary loan requests made in
1974 cleared by the Bibliographical Center for Research in Denver
shows that the load splits neatly into two halves—books from 1900 to
1964 and books from 1965 to date, indicating much greater reliance
on older materials than expected.

Such information tells us only one thing, and that not very comfort-
ing—that we know very little about the factors that cause the use of
specific materials in libraries, and, despite our increasing study of
these dynamics, we have no sounder basis for book selection now than
we did in the past. Therefore, with two feet planted firmly on the void,
I will proceed to tell you what will happen in academic library building over the next ten years.

First, the great force in what we do will not be common sense or
intelligence but sheer lack of funds. Within the rigid jaws of this vise,
which has irrational laws of its own, we may respond, to the degree
that we have choice left, with common sense and intelligence.

The greatest trend, more often by separate libraries rather than in
combination, will be to off-campus storage for lesser used materials.
Candidates for removal will be selected by count of their movement
from the shelves over the year or two preceding storage, and once
again we are in a numbers game. Three movements will be considered
less important than five movements, and we will have no way to determine whether the three movements had greater impact on learning
than the five. This will be one more incursion of accounting methods
into the control of human affairs. I hope that everyone in this audi-

ence is maturely aware that within twenty years we will all be ordered around and supervised, hired and fired, and possibly even married and mated, by bodiless mathematical numbers.

Storage of materials will have the great virtue of removing from the library large numbers of materials that have crept in through loose scrutiny, from gifts, exchanges, and bad selection criteria. However, it has built-in counterproductive forces. When the size of any unit of bookstock, however you may define it, drops below the mass that allows successful location on the shelves of 60 to 70 percent of the items sought, it tends to discourage users from seeking. When a mass of materials becomes difficult to obtain, and for many users delayed delivery is a great difficulty, many instructors will tailor their instruction without material formerly used. The undergraduates will be the great sufferers in this movement; research students and faculty are more persistent.

The second trend in the economics of library building will be the addition to existing buildings, even when they cannot accommodate an addition successfully. In the past many new libraries were built with no thought given to additions as an alternative. We will now swing to the opposite extreme. A good addition must begin with a very good building program, which must program total library needs over the expected life of the combined building AS THOUGH THE PRESENT LIBRARY DID NOT EXIST. Those programs that begin with decisions that Reference will be left where it is, but run over into the present Rare Books area, and Processing will go where Documents is now located are disastrous. These are the alternatives you pay the architect to propose, and like everything else connected with planning libraries, anyone who tries to do the architect's work should be stopped.

In the hands of a sensitive architect, who must then examine the structure and fixed layout of the older building minutely, very unpromising buildings can be added to with great success. I am presently working on two such buildings. The central library at the University of Colorado was built in 1939 as a fixed-function divisional library, with centralized tier-built stacks. It was expanded in 1965 on a budget that prevented the removal of the original load-bearing exterior walls, made of fieldstone a foot and a half thick. As a consequence, no compartment in the building is of the proper size for the function it should perform, overlapping into other areas is commonplace, and important departments are so bafflingly removed from the entrance that they can be found only with the aid of seeing-eye dogs carrying brandy-kegs. You can approach the stacks to begin following the call number sequence at forty-nine different locations. The result is as gruesomely complex and as frustrating.for the user as you can imagine. We are adding 90,000 square feet to it, changing the entrance point and removing tier-built stacks; the result will be a simple building with one totally clear and economical traffic loop on each floor, on which are located all the major components of the library. I am consulting at Ohio State University on a similar addition to a building almost as difficult, and the result is also a radical simplification of the library for the user and a logical combination of its functions.

So, don't rule out an addition until a good architect makes a preliminary review of the problem based on a thorough and detailed building program. On the other hand, there are some notable examples of when not to add. The University of Michigan Library, a bad building to begin with, was added to twice, and the additions were bad each time. Through local campus circumstances impossible to avoid, this building had to be added to a third time, and the final addition is also bad. The University of Illinois central building still has enough adjacent parking space to carry additions to its stack unit for about twenty more years, thus perpetuating the use of a building so difficult to use that even police bloodhounds get lost in it. On the other hand, within recent years, Haverford College added to an ancient library that already had five additions to it, and the result is a highly usable, totally congenial, and charming library, quite suited to the purposes of a small liberal arts college.

The third great force in our future will be lack of energy. In the present social and political dynamics, there will be an increase in underground libraries, to answer the problem of energy consumption. Such libraries pose the problem of any completely interior space, whether above or below ground—how to make them humanly acceptable in feeling. Two underground libraries built to date have been completely successful. The University of Illinois undergraduate library has a large interior court, combined with very high ceilings, thus giving the feeling that the building is not below ground. An even more successful building (in my opinion one of the outstanding libraries on the continent) is at the University of British Columbia, where both sides of the building have been scooped clear and enclosed with glass looking out onto large courts. The result is an underground library that is not underground at all: it merely has a roof that serves as a 75-foot wide central mall.

Energy consumption will, at long last, end the international style of glass, screen-wall buildings. When you think about it, the worst possible place to build glass buildings in the entire United States, because of extremes both of heat and cold, is right at this spot on the shores of Lake Michigan; yet Chicago has more buildings in the international style than any city in the country. It is a style long past its time. On balance a century from now, when people look at the few examples that have not been completely sprayed with asbestos flock covered with polyurethane foam, the international style will be considered the curse of Mies van der Rohe.

Air conditioning will be another victim of the energy shortage. The state of Colorado already has a proscription against its use in new public buildings. In the future buildings will be less comfortable in summer even than those buildings of the recent past with greatly uneven air conditioning. When used, lower air conditioning capacities will be provided in buildings, and temperature control will be a major factor in driving buildings underground. The combination, when it occurs, of underground buildings without air conditioning, especially in wet climates, will be sure to drive patrons away. It will also greatly increase the destruction of paper through mold.

When we do build new libraries, what will be the trend in size over the next ten years? The last three large university libraries built measure 500,000 square feet, 600,000 square feet, and 1 million square feet. The largest, at the University of Toronto, is likely to remain the biggest academic library building in history. That building will remain a monument to the ambitions of a university president who determined that Canada would have one great research library, and that it would be at Toronto. He followed his determination with Niagaras of gold. We recall the year in the recent past when the annual acquisitions of Harvard was surpassed for the first time by upsurgent Toronto, a fact that so shook the confidence of the Brahmins on the Charles River that the next year they wound up eighth in acquisitions in the Association of Research Libraries.

The University of Toronto Library contains one complete floor dedicated to study space for students from other provincial institutions, book capacity for 5 million volumes, and seating for 5,000 students. Its technical processing areas approach the dimensions of Grand Central Station, and while the building cannot accommodate the playing of baseball, with the addition of astroturf, parts of it would make pretty good polo fields. Even its location on campus marks the end of an era of unprecedented academic expansion, which will not be repeated in our lifetime. In anticipation of a large growth to the south, it is located on the southernmost edge of the campus, which now will not spread much past the library. It is safe to predict that we will not see its like again.

For expansion of space, large universities are likely to generate additional branch libraries in special subjects (after all, the inability to add to the central library led to the development of ninety-seven branch libraries at Harvard) and to selective storage. But in the near future, three developments will probably lead to considerable reductions in annual acquisitions, even in the largest research universities, thereby greatly easing the space problem. First, within the next three years, simply because so many scholars and libraries are cutting subscriptions, there should be a noticeable drop in the number of periodicals published.

Second, within the next five years, even the U.S. book publishing industry (which is a very slow learner) will learn the lesson of the automobile industry—when you can't sell them, you have to cut prices. We can cut prices by reducing the size of books from 800 pages to 200, by cutting waste margins and spacing on the page, by using slightly smaller type, and the like. We can stop publishing the remarkable range of weak materials that have spotted recent publications like flyspecks. We can cut prices by ridding the industry of mismanagement, or at least reducing it to the level of mismanagement found in the rest of the country.

Third, within a few years, the beginning of interlocking agreements in collection development, plus the beginning of interconnection of libraries in networks, will make us all feel that we can give up the ingrained idea that we must be independent units. Interlibrary actions will probably not do us that much good, but it will change the mentality of librarians to the extent that they will feel that it is doing a lot of good, and that will change many of our actions.

In the new atmosphere, I think there will actually be exchange of materials from library to library. One library on Long Island, on limited book funds, was developing a fairly extensive collection in the Rumanian language, not because its university was teaching

Rumanian or expected to do so, but because its director thought that no one else in the country was building a Rumanian collection. This library will probably get rid of that collection.

Do I think that microforms will greatly alleviate space demands in libraries? I do not think so over the next ten years. University libraries are already buying less frequently but predictably needed materials in microform in quantity. If the more heavily used materials are bought in microform, libraries will lose in square footage to the reading machines what they will gain in stack reductions. I ran into one case in a library where this had occurred five years ago.

In addition to a decrease in space demands for collections, there will be a decrease in space demands for readers, if we begin to record systematically the peak use of our library seating as a percentage of our student body. There is very little specific information in the literature about the percentage of total students that use the library at one time (outside of the demand for study space during exams, which we should not aim to supply). However, a number of studies record where students do their studying. In defiance of all our experience with dormitories, which are bedlams, all of these studies report that not only do students study most of the time in their dormitories, but overwhelmingly so.

In the mid-1960s, when small liberal arts colleges thought they should plan seats for a third of their students in the library (Oberlin, at one stage of planning, talked about seating 75 percent), I asked the librarian at Amherst how much of their seating was occupied at peak load. (They had planned seats for 66 percent of their students.) He replied that, although they had no systematic record of use, most of their seats were filled a great deal of the time. Some time later I learned that at exactly that time a planning consulting firm working on library problems in that area had done unsystematic random observations of seating in the Amherst library, and had found that at its highest count only 6 percent of the students were using the building.

Somewhat later, this same consulting firm did a systematic count over the entire spring semester, day by day, hour by hour, at a New England college. This was a small, excellent liberal arts college, with a low student-faculty ratio, constant interaction between them, and heavily project-oriented instruction—in short, the dynamics that generate maximum use of a library. Their collection was quite good for their academic program, and the building, though old, was not forbidding inside or out. Their seating capacity was adequate. This seems to be an ideal test of potential student use of libraries. During the entire semester, they found that the peak use, which occurred during only one hour in the entire period, was 11 percent of the student enrollment. This same firm has done thirty similar studies over the past seven years, which show that 11 percent of student enrollment at maximum seating is typical of residential, liberal arts colleges. When I asked why it did not enrich our profession by writing an article about this critical factor, the firm replied that it would hurt their business, because the truth would not delight librarians. No one likes to have his clichés destroyed by information; but if we do our own counting of demand for seating, we will reach similar results. With a changed view of seating and collection needs, I would expect buildings planned in the future to be considerably smaller for any given program than they would have been in the recent past.

How about the computer in libraries? I have commented on the computer in the past, and my conclusions remain the same on the basis of considerably more experience: (1) Good computer programming is one of the rarest skills and very little of it occurs in libraries. (2) Computers still are not cost-effective. (3) Extremely bad library functions are still maintained because they are computerized. Do I expect the use of computers to increase in libraries? Emphatically, yes! How so, in the face of fiscal restrictions? Few people know how to impose cost control accountability on libraries.

There will be two general influxes. First, card production data via OCLC- or BALLOTS-type databases, which can shorten processing time for books in large operations and generally avoid backlogging, at least with the kinds of peak loads we are likely to encounter in the future. The Ohio colleges that have been on-line with OCLC for three years do not think it cost-effective. Everyone else outside who is planning to use it anticipates great cost savings. Second, we will be connected to bibliographical reference data banks, at high cost, when local needs justify the expenditure.

It is extremely easy to accommodate computer terminals in library buildings, by planning a reasonable system of empty electrical conduits in the building.

In summary, the dynamics controlling the building of libraries over the next ten years will be nonhuman rather than human forces. The general result will be to restrict building rather than to expand it. The general effect on buildings will be to ease some of the pressures for building growth and to impair some of the conditions that in successful buildings have made for human comfort in the past. Let me end with a quotation from *The Impact of Technology on the Library Building*, which is as valid today as it was eight years ago when it was written: "It follows, therefore, that library planners can proceed at this time with confidence that . . . developments in the foreseeable future will not alter radically the way libraries are used."

Evan Ira Farber

Limiting College Library Growth: Bane or Boon?

In the past few years I have given a course on the Depression—not the one we're going through now, but THE Depression—focusing on the literature and the arts of the 1930s and going into the economic and political context. In studying and talking about that decade, even while indulging one's nostalgia one cannot help but be struck by the massive unemployment and the accompanying misery and despair resulting from the Crash, and, even more, by the creative responses to them.

The idea of "challenge and response" is hardly a modern notion. Toynbee applied it to entire civilizations, and many writers have individualized it in poems, stories, essays, and aphorisms. "Adversity makes men better," "Are afflictions aught but blessings in disguise?" are a few of the many versions. However one phrases it, perhaps the idea that going through a difficult period can have a salutary effect may be one we should keep in mind. Maybe we will *have to* keep it in mind, if only to preserve our balance. I don't think this is simple rationalization, nor do I mean to sound like Pangloss; this period of economic trauma is surely not the best of all possible worlds. But the present world is, after all, the one we live in, and we should see how we can respond to it creatively and constructively. The economic pressures on higher education are forcing us to take a careful look at what we are doing and why, and *that* can turn out to be a boon.

The space problem has been with us for a long time. Over the past twenty or twenty-five years, however, the years that produced the

modern information explosion and encompassed the period of our
professional lives for most of us, the solutions were relatively easy: ask
for more funds and new buildings, or additions to old ones.
Such solutions are no longer possible. The basic reality now is financial, and we are faced with a shortage of funds not encountered
since the 1930s. The situation today is even more desperate than earlier, for then there was less publishing that we had to keep up with,
and administrative thought had not been shaped by two decades of
affluence and rapid growth. Until a few years ago, we could count on
continuous growth, bigger budgets, foundation grants, and government programs. But now? In 1973, William Jellema, a respected,
conservative authority on the economics of higher education, wrote:
"Within 10 years 30 percent of all private Bachelor's institutions and
limited Master's institutions, 20 percent of the Master's institutions,
and nearly 25 percent of all Ph.D. granting colleges and universities could be ready to go out of business."[1] Lest he be summarily dis-
missed as a doomsayer, you should be aware that since Jellema's book
appeared an average of approximately one college a week has closed
its doors.

Our concerns now must be more than just the price of new buildings or additions to older ones: they are the added costs of maintenance and utilities entailed by the additional space we think we
need, plus the fact that many colleges, rather than increasing the size
of their student bodies, are in fact looking toward decreases. Neither
today, nor in the foreseeable future, can colleges afford that continuing expansion which, not so many years ago, we all took for
granted—and some, I'm afraid, still do. College librarians will have to
assure their administrations that their resources may grow, but that
their buildings will not expand beyond a certain point. But, given the
mind-set of continuing growth, the ever-increasing rate of publishing, and faculty objections to limiting acquisitions, not many librarians have been willing to go out on that limb.

As a first step in solving our problems, we must find new ways of
coping with growth, as well as perfecting and applying ways now used,
but used only sporadically and half-heartedly. Many of us, myself included, have an almost mystical faith in the ability of technology to
cope with new problems and surmount old difficulties. (This faith is
often bolstered by items such as that in the *New York Times* of April
16, 1975, reporting that IBM has developed a rapid printer capable of

over 13,000 lines a minute.[2] On the other hand, this faith is not completely realistic, as is evidenced by our continued dependence on the old, reliable Recordak MPE-1 reader, first used thirty or even forty years ago.) Surely, there will soon be a breakthrough in microform technology which will permit us, at modest expense, to overcome reader resistance to using microforms. (I must confess, though, I have been saying that for years.)

The development of less bureaucratic, more rapid interlibrary loan systems, systems that will guarantee a forty-eight-hour response time to students, is a real need. A number of present delivery systems, proposed systems, and even random ideas can help here, and the development of a rapid and relatively inexpensive telecopier would be of enormous assistance. Access by terminal to a computerized data bank would permit the reduction of much bulky material. For example, the New York Times Information Bank can provide for each library customer a terminal with a high-speed printer that gives abstracts of articles—not merely from the complete files of the *Times*, but presently also from sixty-six other journals. Of course, the service costs $35,000 a year now, plus line time, but it is fairly new and the charge is for a relatively small number of customers. Another example is the number of indexing and abstracting services in the sciences that will become increasingly available through centralized information banks. Think of the space that could be saved just by eliminating files of *Chemical Abstracts* and *Biological Abstracts*.

Compact shelving is a live possibility which few college librarians have considered adequately. This alternative should certainly be considered when building or adding, and, in addition, many of us should also see what areas of our present buildings would be appropriate for the substitution of compact for regular shelving. By appropriate, I mean not only the matter of structural load-bearing, but the factors of space saving and user convenience as well. Saving space or convenience to users may have to be abandoned, but we can no longer afford the automatic luxury of devoting two-thirds of the space in stack areas to seldom-used aisles.

We will have to give increasing attention to weeding, a process that most of us muse over from time to time, and occasionally do, but to which we give little creative thought and less systematically directed energy. Trueswell found that more than 50 percent of the collection at Northwestern could be removed with little impact on the user satisfaction level.[3] On a college level, the percentage would undoubtedly be somewhat smaller, but unquestionably many volumes could be removed with very little subsequent inconvenience to users. Again, part of the problem is our training and experience in building collections. The idea of discarding materials is anathema. After all, many of us became librarians because we love books, and throwing them away, even though they may not have been used in a century, or even consigning them to a regional warehouse, is painful.

Every library school has a course, or part of a course, on acquisitions. How about some time for "de-acquisitions"? Does it take less training or less judgment to know how to weed a collection than it does to add to one? On the contrary, I daresay that more librarians have gotten in trouble by indiscriminate weeding than by indiscriminate purchasing. We have many acquisitions tools; how about some "de-acquisition tools"? College libraries are loaded with titles that were purchased because faculty members wanted research libraries for themselves; because courses were offered once or twice and then dropped; or simply because they were once listed in the Shaw, Lamont or *Books for College Libraries* lists. How about a new ACRL-approved list of titles culled from those earlier lists which could now be dispensed with safely because they have been superseded by time, events, curriculum, or newer publications? I have felt increasingly guilty about one of my own "contributions" to the profession—that is, the list of recommended periodicals (current and retrospective) both in my book and, presently, in our columns in *Choice*. Perhaps we should instead be focusing on periodical files which college libraries could comfortably dispose of, or at least replace with microforms.

All these devices and activities for conserving space would probably cause some inconvenience to users, either in time, space, or format. But we, together with our teaching faculties, must come to realize that not everything can be as it once was; that if we are going to give quality library service to them and to undergraduates, we will still need an adequate staff but the collection and the size of the library cannot grow indefinitely. The college administration is not going to continue increasing that portion of the budget devoted to maintaining a larger, proportionately less used collection, and faculty will have to put up with a certain amount of inconvenience. They will also have to plan ahead a bit more; for example, they can no longer wait until the last minute to select their reserve readings and then raise hell because the library does not have a particular title.

While it is too easy to blame faculty, I do feel that its view of the library as simply a small university library is one of the roots of the present problem. This view is what I have called the "university-library syndrome."[4] It grows out of graduate school training, a training that affects selection of library materials and results in a view of the librarian's role "as a passive one, one devoted to housekeeping, to getting materials quickly and making them accessible . . . and to being available when needed for answering questions, compiling bibliographies, or putting materials on reserve."[5] It does not give the faculty member any sense of the librarian's potential educational role in teaching students how to use the library effectively and independently, in helping them understand the structure of information that a scholar has learned through years of experience and study. Of course, what it results in is most pertinent for us here: the constant demand for more and more acquisitions. To be sure, college librarians have not been unwilling accomplices; in the past, whenever the shelves began to get crowded, they could depend on the Faculty Library Committee to support the move for an addition or a new library.

But before we attempt to re-educate the faculty, we should have a fairly good idea of what materials are used. Most college libraries are handicapped in this respect because of their design, the study and traffic patterns of students in open stack libraries, and circulation systems that do not lend themselves to accurate measurement of use of the collection. The periodicals collection is more susceptible to space saving, and there is less objection to the substitution of periodicals in microform for bound files. However, because in most libraries bound periodicals must be used in the building, their use is difficult to measure. On the other hand, because the periodicals collection is usually centralized and sometimes supervised, some use measurement may be possible. At Earlham, the periodicals collection occupies about one-quarter of our shelving. To decide what titles, or portions of titles, can be substituted by microforms, or even disposed of, we have tried to keep track of use by title and, within title, by decade. If we could close off the periodicals section and fetch each volume wanted, we could have an accurate count. Since we would probably not consider that seriously, we can only estimate use by recording the volumes reshelved, assuming, on the basis of other studies, that about one volume is left unshelved for every three or four used. While rough, this count still gives us some basis for saying to a faculty member: "Look, none of the first fifty volumes of the *American Journal of International Law* has been used in two years. Why can't we just keep the last ten years and depend on interlibrary loan for the others? Or do we really need to subscribe to it at all?" Only rarely has a faculty member scotched the substitution of microform for the original. Sometimes he has even agreed that there really is no need to subscribe to that journal. (In a recent issue of *Microform Review*, there is a good article that treats the practical aspects: costs, space saving, and user convenience.[6])

Why not use citation analysis in such cases? Many studies of citations have determined, with some precision, the relative significance of journals for scholars. That, however, is just the trouble: the needs of undergraduates and of scholars are quite different. In one of his articles in *Science*, Eugene Garfield pointed out that *Scientific American* and *New Scientist* rank very low on the times-cited list, but that "merely means they are written and read primarily for some purpose other than the communication of original research finding."[7] Of course, we all know that *Scientific American* is one of our most frequently used journals, and we would not think of abandoning it simply because it is infrequently cited. A different example is *Fortune*. Our files of *Fortune* are bulky, and those from the 1930s are seldom used. Yet, when I assigned the students in my Depression course to look at an article, "No One Has Starved," in the September 1932 issue, I wanted them not only to read it but to notice the juxtaposition of the article with advertisements for Tiffany & Co., the Packard Club Sedan, or cruises on the Italian or French lines, as well as to appreciate the opulent format, compared with which today's *Fortune* seems pallid. Microfilm would not have accomplished what I wanted, but for a scholar the text of the article alone would probably have sufficed.

My point here is that a college library is very different from a university library, not just in size but also in purpose. Moreover, the needs of college undergraduates have to be determined by different criteria than those used for university students. A college library must have, first of all, a collection of cultural and recreational materials that can expand students' horizons; second, a good basic collection that will meet most of their curricular needs; and, third, a good reference collection that will serve as a key to the immediate library, and to resources elsewhere. Only after these three needs are met should we think about a collection to fill the occasional research need. We should aim for a well-chosen basic collection that meets the first two needs, plus enough advanced materials to meet most of the students' research needs, and then depend on outside sources for the remainder. One implication for space in this connection is that the reference collection cannot be limited by the same criteria as the rest of the collection. But *use* of the reference collection, which is the key to the library's resources (and those outside the library), must be developed. College librarians should be thinking of "reference-centered" libraries, not "book-centered" (that is, warehouse-type) libraries. Every student should know how to use the reference collection, or at least know its potential so he can ask the right questions.

At Earlham, which has a fairly typical curriculum, I have gone out on that limb I spoke about before and have told the administration that, to meet those three needs, a library building for 350,000 volumes should be sufficient for us indefinitely. I am not talking about a steady-state library of 350,000 titles; rather, I am saying that a library accommodating 350,000 volumes in today's terms has sufficient space for continuing growth, albeit at a much, much slower rate. What I am counting on, of course, is that space-saving devices-and technology will permit our future students to have more than 350,000 volumes in the same space as well as fairly quick access to almost anything else they might need.

But what I really want to make sure of is this: assuming that our basic collection is well chosen, our students will make good use of it. A 750,000-volume library sounds good in the college catalog, will assuage any accrediting team, and will please faculty members who are pursuing their own research, but will it really do the freshman or sophomore much good? We should be just as wary of the oversized college library as we are critical of the undersized one. An enormous collection overwhelms, probably inhibits, the beginning student. Moreover, when a college library becomes much larger than necessary, its most important role, education, may have to be sacrificed in order to maintain the seldom-used, or even unused, major portion of the collection.

This is where the "boon" comes in. By being forced to limit collection size, college librarians can devote their resources and energies to doing what a college library should be doing. Too many college librarians have been caught in the university-library syndrome and have thought of their libraries as small university libraries, conscious of only the superficial differences—fewer resources, less scholarly expertise, fewer relationships with other libraries and information centers, and less availability of electronic technology. These differences are limiting, of course, but the one difference between the two types of libraries that we should focus on is that the college library, in contrast to the university library, can establish a unique program, one tailored to the needs and character of its constituency. It has, so to speak, a captive clientele, usually small enough to know as individuals. With that clientele the library can establish as intimate, as helpful, and as educational a relationship as its imagination, energy, and desire allow.

The college library can make many improvements to enhance this relationship, but for me the most important is to teach students how to use the library effectively. Limiting the growth of a library makes it all the more important for students to know bibliographical resources. In most undergraduate research relatively few items *must* be in the library for the work to get done, but the student is not likely to think so. We should help him be imaginative and ingenious as well as efficient in his search, rather than merely diligent in plowing through everything. Students can and should learn to appreciate the importance, even the fascination, of searching for useful materials—that is, to realize that part of their learning is the skill of information retrieval and that such learning entails qualitative as well as quantitative searching. It is here that teaching search strategy becomes important. Moreover, if students are going to have to go outside the library's own collection for some of their needs, the intelligent selection of materials becomes crucial, and only by using the bibliographical apparatus can those selections be made intelligently. This is certainly obvious with terminals to an information bank. If students do not know the structure of indexing vocabulary—another objective of bibliographic instruction—a search through the computer can be very expensive.

Faculty should be willing to accept the concept of a trim collection as long as students use that collection really well and as long as there is relatively quick access to other sources. Without doubt, students can thereby improve their performance, and most faculty should be willing to make the tradeoff of a more limited collection for better work in their courses. But there needs to be some additional re-education of faculty, so that rather than accept term papers that can be done overnight, they should insist on preliminary bibliographies and rough drafts and evaluate the quality of their students' sources as well as their spelling and footnote form.

The library can also help the college in practical ways: to a minor extent, by raising funds from donors or by grants; and to a somewhat larger extent, by saving money through efficient operation. The library can usefully help, though, by enhancing the college's appeal to prospective students. The answer given by the Carnegie Commission on Higher Education to the financial problems of the liberal arts colleges, is not simply to cut costs or cater to the changing needs of students. Rather it said that each college should define its unique educational character and role, and then develop its program to make that character and role a reality.[8] It is here that, by realizing its educational potential, the library can make a real contribution to its college's quality and character.

This contribution can be a significant one and will be in the library's self-interest.In noting the economies that educational institutions will have to make, the Carnegie Commission felt that perhaps one-third of them could be made by fairly obvious efficiencies, but that the other two-thirds would require hard policy choices.[9] If libraries are not to suffer from these "hard choices," they will have to make themselves much more important factors in the college programs, and this is really what I am pleading for. Nothing I have said is very new, but it needs retelling for the urgency is greater now.

Candide, you will remember, finally found out that contrary to what Pangloss had taught him, this was not the best of all possible worlds. But after all his tribulations, his final words to Pangloss were positive ones: "Let us cultivate our garden." Let us cultivate *ours*; let us use these pressures not to act defensively or to retrench, but to do now what we should have been doing all along.

Notes

1. William W. Jellema, *From Red to Black? The Financial Status of Private Colleges and Universities* (San Francisco: Jossey-Bass, 1973), p. 23.
2. *New York Times*, p. 62.
3. Richard W. Trueswell, "User Circulation Satisfaction vs. Size of Holdings at Three Academic Libraries," *College and Research Libraries* 30 (May 1969): 204-213.
4. Evan Ira Farber, "College Libraries and the University-Library Syndrome," in Evan Ira Farber and Ruth Walling, eds., *The Academic Library: Essays in Honor of Guy R. Lyle* (Metuchen, N.J.: Scarecrow Press, 1974), pp. 12-23.
5. Ibid., p. 17.
6. Frederick C. Lynden, "Replacement of Hard Copy by Microforms," *Microform Review* 4 (January 1975): 15-24.
7. Eugene Garfield, "Citation Analysis as a Tool in Journal Evaluation," *Science* 178 (November 3, 1972): 59-60.

8. Carnegie Commission on Higher Education, *Reform on Campus: Changing Academic Programs* (New York: McGraw-Hill, 1972), pp. 36-37.
9. Carnegie Commission on Higher Education, *The More Effective Use of Resources: An Imperative for Higher Education* (N.Y.: McGraw-Hill, 1972), p. 152.

Michael K. Buckland
and
Anthony Hindle

Acquisitions, Growth, and Performance Control Through Systems Analysis

Little critical attention has been devoted to the problem of library size, probably because of the complexity of the issues involved and the difficulties of measurement. This inattention is nonetheless remarkable in view of the substantial capital investment required for chronic building expansion, and the amount of attention that has been devoted to other aspects of librarianship.

This paper explores and explains what appears to be involved in a systems approach to the related problems of acquisitions, growth, and library size. The first part of the paper discusses in general terms some of the relevant factors; the second part examines the potential for mathematical modeling in key areas related to collection size; and the third part considers the effects of decentralization and automation.

Part One: Generalities

OBJECTIVES

Library size is determined by the net effect of the numerous decisions that have been made concerning acquisitions and withdrawals. It would, therefore, seem proper to concentrate on decision-making in libraries and on the impact of decisions on library size.

Decision-making in libraries is complicated by several factors, including the following: (1) Historically, the director of libraries has not made decisions unilaterally. (2) As in social services generally, the decisions are made in the interests of the people served rather than the decision-maker(s). In this sense it is a political rather than an economic activity. [1] (3) The decisions are made for a number of different groups with conflicting interests.

In the analysis of planning and decision-making, it is desirable to clarify the objectives being pursued. The more clearly the objectives can be defined, the easier it will be to make plans and decisions and to predict the consequences of pursuing these objectives. For example, if the sole objective were to maximize the number of volumes held, then bigger would be better. In this case there can be no finite optimal library size and little point in further discussion.

In practice, however, the definition of library objectives is far from straightforward. As Orr has pointed out, "library goodness" is an ambiguous phrase that can cover two quite different concepts[2]— quality and value:

1.*Quality*. How good is the service? This question implies that we have some definition of good. Quality is a measure of capability— being good at meeting some actual or potential demand. It is tempting here to fall back on relatively gross measures of resources such as budget or volumes held rather than measures of the capability with respect to a given criterion.

2. *Value*. How much good does it do? This question also implies that we have some definition of good. Value is a measure of beneficial effects, which are very difficult to quantify. In this case the temptation is to impute rational, or at least self-interested, behavior to library users and to infer that the amount of utilization is an indirect measure of beneficial effects.

The choice of objectives is highly relevant to library size, if it can be shown that the pursuit of different objectives, or combinations of objectives, leads to policy decisions that affect library size in different ways. We can explore this matter by examining a selection of library objectives that have been used, or at least proposed. In examining these objectives, we need to consider the impact their adoption may have on the allocation of limited resources.

Collection Completeness. This objective is illustrated by statements such as: "The library's Aristotle Collection has been strengthened by the acquisition of a manuscript Aristotelian commentary by Albert of

Saxony dated 1407."[3] In this sense collection building should constitute a good deal more than the uncritical amassing of volumes. It calls for careful selection, and, more important, implies a notion of completeness with respect to some definable measure, such as materials likely to be useful in the study of Aristotle, or pharmacy, or librarianship. Collection building tends to lead to an emphasis on increasing the number of different titles held; by implication, then, the purchase of duplicates, or any other service, becomes a lower priority item. Collection completeness is likely to be an expensive objective and to result in large libraries.

Document Availability. This objective, which has been given several different names in the literature, can be measured by the probability that users can find the documents they seek when they want them. Because the emphasis is on the actual demand for documents, a high level of availability is achieved by adopting loan and duplication policies appropriate for titles in relatively high demand. This measure is not very sensitive to the acquisition or nonacquisition of titles in low demand. Consequently, libraries with quite a small range of titles can achieve high levels of immediate availability, though they may have to allocate relatively high expenditure for duplicates. However, these duplicates can be discarded as usage declines.[4]

Browsability. Browsing is defined here as more or less purposeful searching, but not for specific titles. It would seem reasonable to increase the suitability of the collection for browsing. One measure of such suitability is collection bias, a term referring to the extent to which the array of books available at any given time is systematically biased in that books in demand will less likely be available than books in low demand. The reduction of collection bias in this case calls for good selection skills (as with collection completeness) and for policies similar to those for immediate availability—loan and duplication policies suitable for titles in high demand, which may require high expenditure for duplicates (which could be discarded as usage declines). But the measure is insensitive to the acquisition or nonacquisition of titles in low demand. Consequently, a high standard of service can be provided in quite small libraries.[5]

That browsability overlaps with both collection completeness and document availability in its policy implications demonstrates the fact that, while different, these two objectives are interconnected.

Circulation. The actual number of loans from a library is a particularly convenient, if rather crude, measure of utilization. For any given user population, circulation can be generally increased by making the library more attractive, through a more pleasant ambience, especially a new building, or improved availability.[6] The size of the library, however, does not appear to be particularly significant.

Reading. Hamburg et al. advocate maximizing the amount of actual reading as an objective.[7] This measure of utilization, commonly referred to as *document exposure*, is nearer to "beneficial effects" than is circulation. A library seeking to maximize document exposure needs to maintain a high circulation by means of a high level of immediate availability but with the emphasis on plentiful duplication rather than short loan periods. Given limited resources, this combination of policies implies that the acquisition of materials in low demand should receive a low priority and that a high level of service can be achieved without a large library.

Awareness. This term is used to connote the users' level of knowledge of pertinent literature or of whether the library possesses the items concerned. Improved awareness, whether by current awareness services, assistance in literature searching, or the provision of reference tools, calls for investment in reference staff, reference works, and, nowadays, the use of computer-based information retrieval services. These retrieval services, such as MEDLINE and the numerous data bases maintained by agencies such as Battelle, Lockheed, and the Systems Development Corporation, are emerging as supplements to rather than replacements of existing expenses.[8] Given a fixed budget, better awareness can be achieved only at the expense of other uses of money, such as collection building. It can also be argued that emphasis on awareness of pertinent literature, regardless of whether the local library holds it, leads to an emphasis on interlibrary loan facilities and a de-emphasis of the importance of the size of the local library.

Clearly, the choice of objectives can, and should, affect policies and budget allocations. It is also obvious that these decisions will affect acquisition and withdrawal activities and will therefore have differing effects on library size. The principal interactions are sketched in Figure 1.

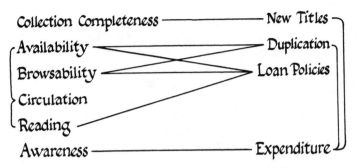

FIGURE 1.   Some interactions in library provision.

Practically every aspect of a library system interacts directly or indirectly with every other. Some of the stronger interactions are shown in Figure 1. The impact of emphasizing any given feature can be traced by following the lines. For example, if *Completeness* is to be stressed, then more *New Titles* are required. This raises *Expenditure* and so, assuming no supplementary funding, it will require less investment in *Awareness* and/or less *Duplication*. However, less *Duplication* will affect *Availability* and *Browsability*, unless compensating adjustments are made to *Loan Policies*. Any impact on *Availability* is likely to affect *Circulation* and, in turn, the amount of *Reading*, depending on what has happened to *Loan Policies*. The lack of a line between two items indicates that the interaction is weak or indirect.

COULD SMALLER BE BETTER?

This conference is concerned with questioning the hypothesis that bigger is better. In reviewing our choices of library objectives, it is convenient to invert the question and ask: Could smaller be better? If we consider a single, centralized library service using manual techniques, we can review the various objectives in the light of this question. If collection completeness is the dominant objective, then it is unlikely that smaller could ever be better. However, if awareness were to become the dominant objective, then the answer would depend on local circumstances. If one picked any "typical" library at random, it is likely that awareness could be improved by means of a reallocation of resources away from collection building and space to reference staff and information retrieval services. Smaller *could* be better with respect to this objective.[9] However, after resources have been reallocated and an "ideal" mix has been achieved, a marginal increase in the range of titles held will improve availability, even though the benefit may be small.

By similar reasoning, we suggest that the answers to the question "Could smaller be better?" are likely to be as follows:

	COULD SMALLER BE BETTER?	
DOMINANT OBJECTIVE	"TYPICAL" LIBRARY	"IDEAL" LIBRARY
Completeness	Unlikely	No
Availability	Yes	No
Browsability	Yes	No
Circulation	Yes	No
Reading	Yes	No
Awareness	Yes	No

In brief, with the probable exception of collection building, it is generally likely that the preferred objective could be better achieved, at least in the short run, by the reallocation of resources and at the expense of growth. However, after reallocation has been achieved, bigger will be expected to be better.

HOW FAR CAN GROWTH BE AFFORDED?

Even if bigger is better, the benefits of being bigger become progressively more expensive to achieve on account of two cost trends: diseconomies of scale and diminishing returns.

1. *Diseconomies of Scale.* A large library can be expected to be more expensive to operate because it is busier: it processes more books and serves more readers. However, it seems reasonable to suppose that the situation is, in fact, worse in that there are diseconomies of scale. In other words, large libraries probably have larger unit costs per book processed, per book held, and/or per service transaction. As the evidence relevant to this contention is meager, we recommend further study on this aspect of library administration.

Authority to support belief in the diseconomies of scale may be found in a report prepared by a Sub-Committee of SCONUL (Standing Conference of National and University Libraries, the British equivalent of the Association of Research Libraries). [10] The Sub-Committee devoted a great deal of study to the possibility of costing particular groups of activity: staffing of service points, seating accommodation, processing activities, and so on. These cost analyses were found to be impractical, but the following conclusion was reached: *"Almost the only constant which emerged from this study was a relationship between the size of a library and the unit cost of both processing and service activities in that library. The larger the one, the greater the other."* (For more detail, see Appendix on page 60).

2. *Diminishing Returns.* The demand for books and journals tends to be concentrated and is highly skewed. In other words, much use is made of a few titles, some use of several titles, and very little use of many more titles. This is the effect of two well-established phenomena: obsolescence and Bradford's Law of Scattering. The implication of this skewed distribution of demand is that the benefits of increasing the number of titles acquired and of retaining titles indefinitely once they have been acquired become progressively smaller insofar as users' demands are concerned.

The combination of diminishing returns and diseconomies of scale makes it clear that even though bigger may be better, bigger becomes costlier. The question then becomes, How far can, or should, bigger be afforded?

A university has various claims on its resources and can hardly be expected to devote everything to library provision. Hence, there must be a finite limit somewhere. (Indeed, the rate of growth of research libraries has diminished in recent years.)

If it is valid to ask whether library provision can become too expensive for the institution, it also seems worth exploring whether library provision might become too expensive for the user. Expense or, more realistically, effort, comes in several forms; for example, distance to the library; time to look items up in the catalog; and time to reach the appropriate part of the stacks. The greater each of these efforts becomes, the more one might expect users to perceive the effort as less worthwhile and to reduce library usage.

In Part One we have endeavored to explore and map out the principal factors that appear to be significant for a systems approach to library size. We can conclude that the problem is complex and that the choice of objective should dominate the allocation of resources.

Part Two: Modeling Aspects of Collection Size

As indicated above, collection size as a decision area interacts with many other decision areas within the library system. Collection size at a given time is also very directly related to collection size at a previous time (in 1974, for example) and to acquisitions, discards, and losses in the intervening time. Such a model is illustrated in Figure 2. In order to effect collection size, we must act upon "acquisition rate" and/or upon "discarding rate." (We will assume that we do not wish to increase losses).

Figure 2 also shows, through dotted lines, the link between the variables of interest and operating costs. It is hypothesized that all of these variables—acquisitions, collection size, and discards—increase costs; large collections are costly, acquisition is costly, and discarding is costly. It is important to note the difference between the arrows emerging from "acquisitions" and from "discards," viz., two "plus signs" versus a "plus" and a "minus" sign. This can be a crucial difference to a librarian because discarding has conflicting effects in the following manner:

Increasing the rate of discarding decreases collection size which decreases operating costs, but it also increases operating costs because of the labor involved. The effect on net cost is uncertain. No such uncertainty exists in the relationship between costs and acquisition rate. Acquiring books both costs money and increases library size. However, it is also worth pointing out the obvious—that collection size can

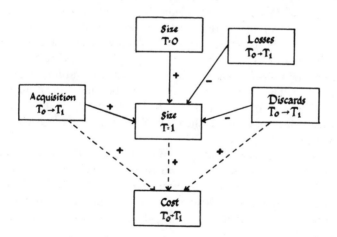

FIGURE 2. The lines and signs indicate the nature of the effects, e.g., discards reduce the size of the library ("minus" effect) but increase library costs ("plus" effect) because of the cost of the labor needed for discarding.

only be reduced by removing more than you add. Thus, it is clearly important to attempt to optimize acquisition and discarding policy, and we shall concentrate upon this issue.

Discarding policy is being examined by B. J. Enright in a current project at the University of Newcastle-upon-Tyne Library, Newcastle-upon-Tyne, England. In this particular case, space constraints necessitated discarding and the problem was simply to determine the required discarding rate in terms of shelf feet per annum and then to select material subject to this requirement. The two variables used to specify discarding priority were age and recorded usage. The type of rule emerging is in the form of two numbers, viz., the number of years since last used and the number of years held. For example 5/20 indicates that material held more than twenty years and not showing any recorded use in the past five years should be discarded. The number of years varies according to the type of material and the subject area. An important aspect of this study is the correlation of recorded and unrecorded use by type of material and subject area. The ratio of the two types of use does vary considerably.

In a current project entitled "Acquisition, Stock Holding, Stock Control and Discarding Policy in Libraries" at the University of Lancaster Library, attention has focused on acquisition policy. From a mathematical viewpoint, acquisition and discarding can be regarded as two sides of the same coin. Both problems become tractable if it can be assumed that any item suggested for acquisition or discard has 'costs' associated with acquisition, nonacquisition, discarding, or retention; and that both user costs and library costs can be quantified. The appropriate decision rules become (1) acquire, if and only if, the costs of nonacquisition exceed the costs of acquisition; and (2) discard, if and only if, the costs of retention exceed the costs of discarding.

The approach is illustrated below for the acquisition of material for which the expected level of subsequent usage is an important criterion of effectiveness. However, for many items worthy of acquisition the expected level of usage will not be the only criterion. Indeed, it may be relatively unimportant, especially when collection completeness is sought.

Provision costs (i.e., library costs) for an acquisition are a function of the direct costs of acquisition—purchase price, processing costs, stock weeding costs—less the interlibrary loan costs saved as a result of acquisition.

An illustrative formulation gives

$$C_T = C_a - [(1 + \alpha) \beta \hat{I} l]$$

where C_T is the total cost of provision,

C_a is the acquisition cost,

the expression in brackets is the saving in interlibrary loan costs,

$\hat{I}$ is the expected level of recorded use over a given time period,

α is the ratio of unrecorded use to recorded use,

β is the proportion of expected demand which would occur even without the presence of the material in the library (The rationale behind this is the assumption that the physical presence of an item in a library tends to generate some demand that might not otherwise have occurred.)

l is the interlibrary loan cost (to the library).

Such a formulation clearly requires a great deal of statistical analysis in order to estimate $\hat{I}, \alpha$, and β, which will be functions of the type of request, the subject area, the type of material, and even the type of requester. Costing the user benefits of an acquisition is even more difficult than estimating provision costs. User benefit costs are regarded as a function of inconvenience and delay costs of interlibrary loan and the benefits of demand generated by the presence of materials in the library. One example of this sort of approach is as follows:

Total user benefit equals the cost savings to the user of avoiding interlibrary loan plus the benefits of generated demand.

$$B_T = (1 + \alpha) \beta \hat{I}(ut) + (1 - \beta) [(1 + \alpha) \hat{I}] l'$$

where ut is the cost to the user of delay in obtaining material (u is user cost per hour, t is time); l' is the benefit of a generated use. The variable l' is used here because at Lancaster the interlibrary loan cost is used as an estimate of this benefit. Such an assumption is not strictly necessary, although it does lead to a simple expression for benefit/cost ratio, viz.,

$$\frac{\text{Benefit}}{\text{Cost}} = \frac{\text{Total expected usage X interlibrary loan cost function}}{\text{Acquisition cost}}$$

$$= \frac{[(1 + \alpha)\hat{l}][\beta(ut) + l]}{C_a}$$

The higher the value of this ratio for any given title, the higher priority for purchase it should be given. For any set of titles, they should be selected in descending order until the budget for acquisitions runs out.

Very similar expressions can be obtained using other assumptions concerning l'. For example, one could proceed on the assumption that all uses tend to have a comparable benefit whether or not generated by the presence of materials. Furthermore, the relative values of the benefit/cost ratio for different titles are not affected by the assumptions concerning l'.

The rate of acquisitions, and hence collection size, will be extremely sensitive to changes in the library budget, especially in the short term. An "expenditure model" constructed at the University of Lancaster[11] gave the results shown in Table 1.

Table 1. Three Levels of Expenditure (in £1,000)

BUDGET	TOTAL	STAFF	BINDING	SUNDRIES	ACQUISITION
1	219.8	121.1	12.7	15.6	70.4
2	296.2	125.0	15.2	15.6	140.4
3	372.6	135.8	17.1	15.6	204.1

In this particular library, the acquisition rate *has* to suffer if the library budget is cut, for it is clearly the most vulnerable area in the short run. Of course, a difficulty of application arises because the requests for acquisition dribble in over time rather than being available as a complete list at the beginning of a time period. There are several possible ways around this problem: (1) Estimating the acceptance threshold from previous years' data (accepting all requests above this estimated threshold) and monitoring the expenditure on acquisition;

fine tuning the threshold as the end of the budget year approaches. The use of a "conditional accept" mechanism helps in this sort of procedure. (2) Extensive use of the approval plan mechanism, whereby material can be kept for a while, carefully appraised, and, in some cases, returned. This approach is very attractive. Not only can the acquisition algorithm operate on lengthy lists at least frequent intervals, but there is also some opportunity to improve the estimate of $\hat{I}$ through closer inspection of the material.

Clearly, *the critical issue* is the user cost parameter (u). Some research has been carried out which attempts to quantify it. For example, Flowerdew and Whitehead [12] review several studies along these lines, and Houghton and Prosser [13] have reported some findings. At Lancaster the approach thus far has been to impute u from past behavior for the *total* collection and to use this value to control *allocation* of the acquisition budget between competing demands for acquisition.

Other terms in the expression are problematical. For example, even C_a presents difficulties because it is probably not a linear function of the number of items acquired. The purchase price is simple enough but there may be diseconomies of scale affecting processing costs and holding costs. In fact, any such diseconomics might also affect user costs and, hence, the term (ut) in the benefit expression. (The possibility of diseconomies of scale has been mentioned above.)

From first principles one can theorize that any activity that involves searching will require more effort per search in a large file or bookstack than in a small one. For example, one can draw the analogy with information processing. If you do not know what day it is but someone offers you a situation whereby any question you ask will be answered "yes" or "no" (truthfully), the best strategy is to divide alternatives into equal groups as far as possible, e.g., "is today Monday, Tuesday or Wednesday?" If Yes, then "is it Monday or Tuesday?" The number of search steps is given by log (base 2) of N, where N is the number of possible answers. More generally, the number of steps is given by

$$-\sum_i p_i \log_2 p_i$$

where p_i is the probability of the ith signal.

In the equal probability case (and, typically, in the more general case), the expected search cost (per search)—the number of stages—is a monotonically increasing function of N. Little attention appears to have been paid to the possible diseconomies of scale in libraries. However, in a study of overlap in holdings of libraries by the University of Lancaster Library Research Unit,[14] some data on search times for individual items in catalogs of various sizes were obtained in order to estimate the cost of the study. The sample was composed of a well-edited and alphabetized list of (mainly) little-held monographs, all of which were from the same part of the catalog. The searching was done by expert searchers. The results are shown below in Table 2. In this particular case, the diseconomy is even more marked than a logarithmic function would suggest.

Table 2. Search Times

CATALOGUE SIZE (MAIN ENTRIES FOR MONOGRAPHS)		SEARCH TIME PER ITEM. (IN SECONDS)
1	100,000	12
2	500,000	18
3	3.5 million	60

If a benefit-cost ratio is obtained for a library and if it is implemented for both acquisitions and (with appropriate modification) discarding, the library will, by definition, be a library of optimal size. This notion of optimal size holds a certain fascination for librarians and operations researchers. It is particularly appealing to the librarian if the optimal library turns out to be larger than he can afford with his current budget. However, it is important to recognize that the optimal size is dynamic (i.e., it changes over time) and is not a single number. Nevertheless, if the quality of material available for acquisition remained constant, if the obsolescence rate were stationary, if the user population had constant characteristics, and so on (i.e., if all exogenous variables were stationary), there would be an expected value for the optimum size variable. It would clearly be of considerable use if we were able to estimate this parameter. Thus far, attempts to perform this estimate have been extremely rudimentary, and only tentative models have been suggested (cf. Buckland[15] and Douglas[16]).

In addition to the difficulties of user cost and the diseconomies of scale, previous work has floundered on the selectivity question. Even a library with a highly sophisticated acquisition and discard system will not have the optimal set of material at any instant in time. No librarian, if his library were burnt to the ground, would buy back his previous selections. Common sense dictates that all material acquired will be kept a reasonable number of years before being considered for discarding, and obsolescence will take its toll. Any model (such as the Douglas model) based on the assumption of a perfectly selected collection is of little practical value.

Mathematically, the problem appears extremely complex, and the only feasible approach is to construct a simulation model in which collection size emerges from the interplay of (alternative) acquisition and discard systems. Of course, obsolescence will still need to be modeled and "search" costs must be treated as increasing with library growth.

Part Three: Restructuring the System

As we explore the economic limits of library size, it is necessary to consider whether some organizational or technological restructuring of the system might permit the avoidance or, at least, the mitigation of the problems of library size. Two responses will be considered: decentralization and automation.

1. *Decentralization.* The change from a centralized to a decentralized library service system will necessarily restructure the pattern of costs: both the costs of provision and the costs (effort) required of the users. These costs appear to fall into two broad categories that react differently to decentralization:

Searching costs are, in general, reduced. This class of costs includes the distance that the user has to travel to reach the library containing the needed item. This is true in a probabilistic way. It is likely (but not certain) that most users (but not all) will need to expend less effort on most (but not all) occasions. A similar reduction can be expected in searching in catalogs, seeking items in the stacks, and reshelving and filing circulation records. It is less work to file (or pull) ten items from each of ten files of 1,000 records than to file (or pull) one hundred items from one file of 10,000 records.

Queuing costs, however, increase. This class of costs includes much of the reader services staffing of libraries, the provision of seating, and the duplication of titles. It is less expensive to handle a given number of inquiries if they all come to one inquiry desk than if they are distributed over several separate inquiry desks. It is much more expensive to have a set of *Chemical Abstracts* at each of five different libraries than it is to have one or even two sets at a central science library. The net effect of these two conflicting cost trends will depend on the local situation. They might even balance each other out, but we can be sure that the cost structure will have changed. (Some work, most of it theoretical, has been done on the size and viability of branch libraries, e.g., Woodburn,[17] Brookes,[18] Coughlin,[19] and Pitt.[20])

2. *Automation.* The effect of shifting from manual to computer-based techniques will be discussed in more detail by William Corya and Michael Buckland (see pp. 131-140). For the present discussion, it can be said that automation changes the behavior of the searching class of costs. Whereas manual searching costs are rather directly dependent on the size of the file being searched, with computer-based searches this dependency appears to be lessened. In an extreme case, a library whose holdings are recorded in a cooperative bibliographical data base, such as the Ohio College Library Center (OCLC), would find that the search cost is influenced by the number of titles recorded at OCLC but is substantially independent of the size of the library making the search.

Summary

Our exploration of what appears to be involved in a systems approach to acquisitions, growth, and library size has led to several conclusions: the problems are complex; the pursuit of objectives ought to dominate the decision-making and the allocation of resources. Growth and library size are determined *indirectly* by these decisions; while acquisitions and discarding determine library size, they have different effects on costs and space; there appear to be diseconomies of scale; a direct approach to optimal library size is likely to be misguided; dynamic control mechanisms are needed, based on objectives, plans, and management information; and restructuring the mode of provision by means of decentralization or automation will have different effects on different classes of costs.

Notes

1. Sir G. Vickers, *The Art of Judgement: A Study of Policy Making* (London: Chapman & Hall, 1965).
2. R. H. Orr "Measuring the Goodness of Library Services: A General Framework for Considering Quantitative Measures," *Journal of Documentation* 29, no. 3 (September 1973); 315-332.
3. University of Toronto Library, *Annual Report of the Chief Librarian*, 1972-1973, p. 5.
4. For a detailed discussion, see Michael K. Buckland, *Book Availability and the Library User* (New York: Pergamon, 1975), especially Chapter 7.
5. Ibid.
6. Ibid., Chapter 9.
7. M. Hamburg et al., *Library Planning and Decision Making Systems* (Cambridge, Mass.: MIT Press, 1974).
8. J. J. Gardner et al., "The Delivery of Computer-Based Bibliographical Search Services by Academic and Research Libraries," *ARL Management Supplement* 2, no. 2 (September 1974).
9. Much depends on the way space costs are handled. Traditionally, space costs are not chargeable to the library's budget. To use C. F. Carter's phrase, space is, in effect, "either free or not available." Yet it must be costing somebody something. Note also that *economic* costs are not the same as those used by cost accountants. Cf. A. D. J. Flowerdew and C. M. E. Whitehead, *Cost-Effectiveness and Cost/Benefit Analysis in Information Science* (London: London School of Economics and Political Science, 1974). (OSTI report 5206). Available from British Library Lending Division, Boston Spa, Wetherby, West Yorkshire, England.
10. Great Britain, University Grants Committee, Committee on Libraries, *Report* (London: HMSO, 1967), ("Parry Report"), Appendix 9: Supplementary SCONUL Report of the Sub-Committee on Standards in University Libraries, p. 278.
11. M. G. Simpson, *Planning University Development; Studies in Institutional Management in Higher Education, University of Lancaster* (Paris: Organisation for Economic Cooperation and Development, 1972).
12. Flowerdew and Whitehead, *Cost-Effectiveness and Cost-Benefit Analysis.*
13. B. Houghton and C. Prosser, "A Survey of the Opinions of British Library Lending Division Users in Special Libraries on the Effects of Non-immediate Access to Journals," *Aslib Proceedings* 26, no. 9 (September 1974): 354-366.
14. University of Lancaster, Library Research Unit, *National Catalogue Coverage Study: Report to the National Libraries ADP Study* (Lancaster, England: University of Lancaster Library, 1971). Available from the British Library Lending Division, Boston Spa, Wetherby, West Yorkshire, England as: NAB 800-N, *The Scope for Automatic Data Processing in the British Library. Supporting Paper N: National Catalogue Coverage Study.* M. K. Buckland, A. Hindle, and G. P. M. Walker, "Methodological Problems in Assessing the Overlap Between Bibliographical Files and Library Holdings," *Information Processing and Management* (forthcoming).

15. M. K. Buckland, *Book Availability and the Library User*, Chapter 2 and Appendix A.

16. I. A. Douglas, "Optimum Size of a Library of Monographs," *Australian Library Journal* (November 1973): 404-407.

17. I. Woodburn, "A Mathematical Model of a Hierarchical Library System," in A. G. Mackenzie and I. M. Stuart, eds., *Planning Library Services: Proceedings of a Research Seminar, Lancaster, 1969*. University of Lancaster Library Occasional Papers, 3, (Lancaster, England: University Library, 1969). (ERIC Report ED 045 173.)

18. B. C. Brookes, "The Design of Cost-Effective Hierarchical Information System," *Information Storage and Retrieval* 6, no. 2 (June 1970): 127-136; and B. C. Brookes, "The Viability of Branch Libraries," *Journal of Librarianship* 2, no. 1 (January 1970): 14-21.

19. R. D. Coughlin, F. Taïeb, and B. H. Stevens, *Urban Analysis for Branch Library System Planning* (Westport, Conn.: Greenwood Press, 1972).

20. W. B. Pitt, D. H. Kraft, and L. B. Heilprin, "Buy or Copy? A Library Operations Research Model," *Information Storage and Retrieval* 10, no. 9/10 (September/October 1974): 331-341.

Acknowledgment: The project at the University of Lancaster Library Research Unit entitled "Acquisition, Stock Holding, Stock Control and Discarding Policy in Libraries" is under the direction of Mr. A. Graham Mackenzie, University Librarian, University of Lancaster, Lancaster England. The study of stock control at Newcastle-upon-Tyne University, England, is under the direction of Dr. B. J. Enright, University Librarian, Newcastle-upon-Tyne University, Newcastle-upon-Tyne, England. Both projects are supported by the British Library Research and Development Department (formerly the Office for Scientific and Technical Information).

APPENDIX: Extract from the Supplementary Report of the Sub-Committee on Standards in University Libraries.

8. A great deal of study was devoted to the possibility of costing particular groups of activity. Attempts were made, for instance, to work out a formula for the staffing of service points; but it was found that conditions differ too radically to make this possible. Variables include the quality and amount of seating accommodation in relation to student and staff members, the siting of the library in relation to traffic routes, the traditional patterns of library use, reliance on branch and departmental libraries or on other local resources such as public or learned society libraries, the charging system used, the regu-

lations governing loans, division of labour among the staff, and hours of opening. A similar attempt to cost book-processing activities (acquisition, cataloguing, classification) was frustrated by the wide variation in systems used and in methods of organizing the work, as well as by the arbitrary limitations imposed by the design of buildings and such factors as the accessibility of the catalogue. *Almost the only constant which emerged from this study was a relationship between the size of a library and the unit cost of both processing and service activities in that library. The larger the one, the greater the other.*

9. This conclusion may seem to indicate inefficient management, since it runs counter to general experience in industry and commerce. But the economies of large scale enterprise in these fields are due in large measure to the greater standardisation which it makes possible, to the development of bulk purchasing methods and of mass production techniques, and to the scope afforded for rational division of labour. The nature of library service is very different. Whatever the size of the unit, its activities remain for the most part "one-off" transactions; the purchase of a single copy of a book, the making of an individual record of that book, the location of a particular item of information for an individual reader. None of these is susceptible to bulk-handling techniques and the economies which they offer; on the contrary, all continue to involve individual search in catalogues, indexes and other types of record, or on the shelves, which inevitably becomes slower as the bulk of the records increases and as the area occupied by the collection grows. True the large unit can make greater use of unskilled or semi-skilled staff for routine duties; but much (if not all) of the resulting saving is offset by the necessary transfer of senior staff from productive work to new activities of supervision and organization. In the world of university libraries the true benefits of greater size are found not in more economical operation but in greater serviceability to the user, who has access to a richer pasture.

Marvin Scilken

Solving Space and Performance Problems in a Public Library

The Orange (New Jersey) Public Library was founded in 1884, and its present building was erected in 1900. It owns 100,000 adult volumes representing 80,000 titles and adds 5,000 volumes each year. The total adult circulation was 140,000 in 1974.

What is described here are systems of performance and nongrowth developed in a public library serving a heterogeneous community of 33,000 people. Orange has one of the highest tax rates in the state of New Jersey and a fairly low family income level. Nine dollars were spent per capita for all operations in 1974. The library participates in a well-developed (daily truck delivery) network of interlibrary loans with neighboring public libraries. The network extends through the great Newark Public Library to the State Library and two major university libraries. In 1974 (all statistics in this paper are for 1974) 750 items were borrowed from other libraries. Most were borrowed from neighboring public libraries, with only a very small number coming from the State Library and the university libraries.

A one-day (statistically invalid) survey done with the assistance of the Rutgers University Bureau of Library Research indicated that 431 people visited the library. Eighty percent of them reported they were "satisfied"; 44 percent were "students"; and 25 percent indicated they were not card-carrying users.

The staff at the library feels that about half the loans it initiates are for college students who cannot or do not choose to get their books from their college libraries.

Performance

The Orange Library tries to satisfy as many people as possible for, as public librarians, we constantly have to sell our services. We do not have a captive audience. We cannot be certain the books we buy will be used. We do not know what subjects will be in demand. For our $300,000 budget we have to compete with garbage collection, the police department, the fire department, and other public services. We must satisfy a large percentage of our users, and maintain acceptance by nonusers, to assure our continued support.

Public libraries have no accrediting agencies to insist on standards, but the state of New Jersey offers "a carrot, but not a stick" type of guidelines.

The Orange Public Library does not consider itself a research library. We cannot be with our size or $9.00 per capita support (or assuming we serve 30 percent of the population, about $30 per user). If we were a research library we could not serve the needs of our users and potential users, for there are very few unattached scholars in Orange. Of course, this situation may change with the growth of adult independent education, but so will our costs. Who is to pay for the type of library service needed by unattached college students remains to be seen.

With experience, I have come to the view that public library operations are a peculiar form of retailing. We hope to have as many returns as we have "sales." Public library turnover is quite high. Some small public libraries actually turn over their collections six times a year; that is, their circulation is six times their holdings. Some public libraries rent for circulation to their public new books that they do not wish to add to their permanent collection.

Early in my library career I discovered that what most adult library users want is recently published books. We decided to meet this demand by *buying early, getting books on the shelf quickly,* and *buying enough copies.* When buying in the public library field, one usually has a review or other good reason for buying. Publishers help by advertising books that are selling and not advertising books that do not sell. Most new books in a public library have short lives, and the period of their most active life is right after publication.

The Frontlog System[1] was developed so that books could be circulated with full circulation control, within a day or two of their arrival at the library, before the receipt of catalog cards and with very little additional work.

We have been unable to revive interest in many older books. For instance, a book about the German cruiser *Emden*, a true adventure story of World War I which was published five or six years ago with an attractive jacket and circulated well at that time, was again placed on our "New and Popular" nonfiction shelf in the hope that it might circulate. But readers avoided it and all but a few of the other old books promoted in this manner. Readers seem to have a mysterious sense that helps them avoid older books.

We try not to make our borrowers wait more than one month for a book, though even that may be too long. To meet this standard, we once purchased fifty-seven copies of a particular title. In most cases, however, six or seven copies of the very few titles that are most in demand will enable us to meet the one-month standard.

In most public libraries, books in heavy demand are never seen on the shelf. To show that the library actually owns the books, we maintain a "rental" collection with the first three days free. These books have a high borrowing and return velocity and reduce the number of reserves. Reserves are labor-intensive and cause books to be under the desk rather than being read during the most useful period of their lives.

Multiple copies, of course, present a problem when demand wanes. This problem, among others, prevents many librarians from buying sufficient copies to keep reserve periods reasonable, if any reserve period can be termed reasonable. We gradually remove multiple copies. Suitable ones we place in our "Read and Return" Collection[2] (in doctors' offices, banks, etc), for people who will not or cannot make it to the library to "read and return."

To determine what we need in addition to the obvious best sellers, we use a system devised by Brian Smith and John Foresman, "The Always Available Book System."[3] For this system we have identified some 500 to 1,000 books that we wish to have generally available. The list is compiled from best seller lists, reserves, interlibrary loans (our own and requests from other libraries), hunches, books lost in circulation, and so forth. These titles are put on cards (Figure 1) which are used to check what is on the shelves. Best sellers are checked weekly, and others once a month or so. Non-best seller titles not found for two or three months are reordered. Best seller reorders are determined by the number of reserves and copies on the shelf list.

FIGURE 1. *The "Always Available" form designed and used at The Orange Public library. The top lines indicate the year and month the book was looked for; COS represents "copies on shelf." To order, three copies of the form are made on a photocopy machine and used as order forms.*

The integrity of the collection is also maintained through use of a combined overdue notice and reorder form. The form notifies a borrower of an overdue item and may also be used to reorder in case of nonreturn. The theory is that a book that was borrowed and in print may be wanted by others and therefore is a good candidate for replacement. Great care must be used here for it has been found that many such replacements do not circulate well enough to justify replacement costs.

Whenever possible we replace missing books with quality paperbacks. The smaller format allows us to cram more books within the same shelf space. Moreover, many quality paperbacks withstand moderate circulation as well as hardback trade books.

Growth

As a neophyte librarian I was surprised to find that weeding was far more difficult than buying. I do not recall that library school placed any emphasis on weeding, though many courses dealt with book selection. Weeding should be given a major place in the library school curriculum, for it is a far more amorphous art than book selection.

While our aim is to discard one book for every book we buy, we have not been able to meet the standard. Last year we added 8,000 books and discarded only 4,500. We have been able to live with this. No doubt we have shrinkage. We estimate that about 1 to 2 percent, or about 1,000 to 2,000 books, are stolen each year.

Barrow Laboratories has done a disservice to public libraries with its development of *permanent* catalog cards. Since we view most books and other materials as only temporary residents of the library, we need a catalog card that will disappear without a trace after five years. Perhaps Barrow Laboratories can develop a series of self-destruct cards with lives of one, two, three, five, and ten years. If a library wished to keep a book after the self-destruct period, it would have to recatalog it. After this period of time, new and more relevant subject headings and/or class numbers might be required. Raganathan said that libraries are living organisms. By necessity we at the Orange Public Library have checked the limit of our growth but not our development. We try to maintain a sleek appearance in spite of our age.

The object of every library should be to buy the books it needs and to exclude the books it does not need. While we all seem to want at least one copy of books we need, we have generally not paid enough attention to excluding books we do not need. To state Scilken's Law of Librarians' Science: librarians much prefer buying books that no one wants to books they know everyone wants; or, it's better to serve a potential reader tomorrow than an actual reader today. By implication, it has been suggested that a library should include one copy of every recent book published.[4] The more titles a library has, this theory seems to say, the nearer to heaven the library is. On the other hand, the noted biologist Garret Hardin has submitted in his wonderful story "The Last Canute"[5] that the older and larger the library the worse it is, for it holds only the books that readers have not found fit to steal.

The Molesworth Institute[6] has suggested that libraries could achieve negative growth simply by replacing their book return chutes with paper shredders. The money saved in not cataloging books (books are arranged in author order on the shelves), not controlling circulation, and not expanding the building would be put into the purchase of new books. The Institute opined further that the faculty would have to update its reading lists and thinking. Unfortunately, this solution shreds the books that are being used. The

Molesworth Institute should devise a system that would shred the unread books and laborlessly pull the unneeded catalog cards.

For weeding purposes, we used to check *Books for College Libraries, The Lamont Catalog, Standard Catalog Series,* and the like. We no longer do so because it is too time-consuming, and, moreover, we found that a listing in these catalogs was no indication of future demand.

We also used to keep previous works of currently active authors, hoping that people reading the latest work might wish to read some of the earlier ones. Since we found very little demand, we now weed these as well.

Even before we found that Trueswell supplied a firm basis for belief, we acted upon the theory that date of last use was generally the best prediction of future use. Because we use transaction card photographic charging, there is no automatic record of a book's past use, and staff time cannot be spared to examine every book. Other techniques have been devised to winnow books for possible discard.

Since 1963 we have been noting the date of return in the book and since 1967 we have been stamping the date of return on the book pocket. A different color is used for each year. With this crude system, the book carries its own record of its circulation. In the case of multiple copies, it is difficult to determine the total circulation of a title.

In order to maintain the accuracy of our records, books are stamped (with a slightly different date stamp) when they are found misshelved or otherwise appear to have been used. A recent study at the Orange Public Library indicated that a substantial portion of our circulation might occur within the library. In-library circulation, of course, eludes most circulation records. Therefore, our stamped records cannot be applied mechanically. We do plan to try to record in-library circulation by asking users to write in the date of use.

For weeding purposes, pages are asked to pull or turn down books without current stamps. Depending on the subject area, two to four years of apparent nonuse will provide candidates for discarding. These books are then examined by a professional for possible discard.

In addition to the stamped dates, several external clues are used as a basis for selection for possible discard. The year of cataloging is noted in small type on call number labels. The general period of acquisition can frequently be ascertained by other external clues—different jackets, different labels, different type on the call number labels. These are, of course, only assists; one must still use one's judgment and/or guesses.

Another technique used to purge the catalog and shelves is to file subject cards by date of publication with the latest first. This method, first designed for the benefit of the reader, now assists the library in weeding. By filing subject cards in this manner, a group of "old" cards is gathered at the end of the subject heading file. Depending on the subject, most cards are removed beyond an arbitrarily selected year. We pull the cards and search for the book; if the book is found, we ask ourselves if it should be retained. If we decide to keep the book, the current date is stamped on the face of the catalog card so that it will not be pulled again for a few years, and the card is returned to the front of the file.

Most books that are found are considered for discarding (applying Hardin's idea, "Why hasn't it been stolen after forty years?"). Books not found are searched for three times and are then written off or re-ordered. Since we will buy almost any book in the catalog that is requested, most of those not found are apparently gone and forgotten. Before we came to this conclusion, we purchased a few that were in print, some from reprint publishers. In almost all cases circulation did not justify their cost. Our experience should serve as a warning to be cautious of reprint publishers' wares. Replacements purchased from trade publishers did better but not overwhelmingly so.

Inventory is rarely taken at the library, and the charging system does not give an ordered record of what is in circulation. We can only tell what has not been returned. Public librarians generally have not felt it was worth the expense to be able to tell where every book is at every moment. Why should we spend a lot of money to find out where a book is if it may be impossible to retrieve?

With the book actually in hand, our primary retention criterion is use of the book; to a lesser degree we consider the author and the subject. (No matter how little they have been used until now, we are not discarding anything of Bicentennial interest. In fact, we are adding "Bicentennial" subject cards to the catalog for older items.)

Since we do not have access to subject specialists or faculty, we use a generalist to examine our potential discards for subject, authorship, and possible value. For effective weeding, the weeder must know the number of times a book circulated, its date of last circulation, and whether the book was available for circulation. The person who buys should be the person who weeds.

For some standard books that have been weeded, we leave the cards in the catalog with an overlay (see Figure 2). These books are considered "gone but not forgotten."

After applying this technique to discarded books, we now apply it to new books. Working on the assumption that cards in the catalog require less room than actual books on the shelf, the "buy the card but not the book" system was developed.

When a book gets an "every library should have" review, but, deep in my heart I know it won't move, we buy and file the cards but not the book. Then, if the book is requested, we buy or borrow it. We are, in effect, pre-weeding. A front page review in the *New York Times Sunday Book Review* for a two-volume work on the Mediterranean at $37.50 is a good candidate for our "buy the cards but not the book" collection. This highly touted, probably important, book would very likely not circulate enough to justify its cost. Buying the cards would minimize the "tsk-tsk" effect when visiting librarians look into the catalog to evaluate the collection. The important thing is that readers are reminded that the book does exist and that it can be obtained for them.

In many libraries there is little congruence between books listed in the catalog and books available for immediate use. Cards in public li-

---

ASK THE LIBRARIAN TO GET THIS BOOK FOR YOU

Dickinson, Robert Eric, 1905–
    Germany; a general and regional geography. ₁1st ed.₁ New York, Dutton, 1953.

    xx, 700 p. illus., maps. 23 cm. ₁Dutton advanced geographies₁
    Bibliography: p. 666–685.

MENTION THAT IT IS IN THE
"OUT-OF-LIBRARY COLLECTION"

1. Germany—Descr. & trav.—1945– Germany.　　2. Physical geography— Germany.

DD43.D5　　　　　　914.3　　　　　　52–12956
Library of Congress　　　₁15₁

FIGURE 2.　Clear plastic overlay (with red lettering) on card indicates book has been weeded but cards have been left in the catalog for our "gone but not forgotten" books. The same overlay form is used when cards are ordered for "pre-weeding."

brary catalogs represent items that have passed through the catalog department at one time or another. They may be lost, stolen, or chewed by a dog. Libraries with book catalogs, where most locations are not given, have a similar lack of congruence, as do college libraries that file other libraries' holdings in their catalogs.

By not purchasing books we are urged to buy, we have merely added another dimension. The money saved by this pre-weeding is put into duplicating items that really are in demand, and we are thereby able to serve our actual readers better.

The number of "pre-weeded" and "gone but not forgotten" titles is very small. The Orange Public Library's readers have a good chance of finding the overwhelming number of books listed, or at least those books purchased within the last twenty years.

Why, then, should these cards be placed in the catalog? Though we try to obtain any book that can be verified, readers tend to request titles that are listed in the catalog. The full set of cards provides author, title, and subject access. If we guess wrong, we buy the book; perhaps by that time we can pick up a remainder. One obvious limitation of the "gone but not forgotten" and "pre-weeding" approach is that the reader seeking these books may have to wait more than the normal time to obtain them.

There is a paradoxical situation in most libraries: users have immediate access to books they do not want (unpopular books) and delayed access to books they do want (popular books). The "pre-weeding" and the "gone but not forgotten" approach tends to resolve this paradox by releasing funds for purchasing more copies of high-demand titles. This Gogolian approach to collection building, if carried through, could provide collections of maximum usefulness to most users while minimizing some of the costs in acquiring "dead books."

If "pre-weeding" catches on, it will have some interesting ramifications. Just as reprint publishers brought many books into print without actually printing them, merely by listing them in their catalogs, perhaps many books will be "published" only in catalog card form.

The "pre-weeding" approach pays only if the librarian uses good judgment in selecting "pre-weeds." The cost of not buying the books should obviously not exceed the cost in lending "pre-weeded" books by interlibrary loan. A careful comparative study of costs is indicated.

One indicator of the effectiveness of the Orange Public Library's approach to solving growth and performance problems is the fact that its per capita loan rate (among adults) exceeds that of all other libraries serving similar communities in New Jersey, although it continues to occupy a building that was erected 75 years ago, when book production was a fraction of what it is today. While a library must continuously modify the composition of its collections to meet constantly changing demands, our experience shows that, contrary to the conventional wisdom, successful performance does not necessarily require continuous expansion of library collections and buildings. Adaptation, not growth, may be the better answer to a library's performance problems, as well as the least expensive.

Notes

1. Marvin H. Scilken, "Backlog to Frontlog," *Library Journal* (September 15, 1969): 3014.
2. Marvin H. Scilken, "Read and Return Collection," *Wilson Library Bulletin* (September 1971): 104.
3. Brian Smith, "The Always (Almost Always) Available Book System," *The U*N*A*B*A*S*H*E*D Librarian*, No. 5 (Fall 1972): 3.
4. Ernest R. De Prospo et al., *Performance Measures for Public Libraries* (Chicago: ALA, 1973), pp. 34-35.
5. Garret Hardin, "The Last Canute," in James V. McConnell, ed., *The Worm Returns* (Englewood Cliffs, N.J.: Prentice Hall, 1965), p. 103 ff. Originally appeared in *The Scientific Monthly* in 1946.
6. Norman Stevens, "Negative Library Growth," *The U*N*A*B*A*S*H*E*D Librarian*, No. 13 (Fall 1974): 6.

Richard W. Trueswell

Growing Libraries: Who Needs Them?
A Statistical Basis for the No-Growth Collection

The term "no-growth collection," as I use it here, needs to be clari-
fied at the outset. Let me first say what it is not: it is not a library collection where new-book purchases cease, and it is not a library where
purchases of necessary duplicates are suspended. However, it is a library where the total number of monographs is held at a no-growth
value close to, if not at, the holdings capacity of the library itself.

The no-growth collection attempts, as a matter of policy, to satisfy a
stated percentage of total circulation demand, with the understanding that the remaining percentage of nonsatisfied demand will be met
through another library or through a cooperative storage facility that
houses only lesser used materials.

I should note that my research is directed to inanimate objects in
the library, namely the collections, and that my view regarding library personnel is one of great esteem. I have always found librarians
to be extremely helpful in solving the complex problems involved in
my research. These comments are meant to emphasize that the author
is critical only of the holdings that serve the user, not the people.

Perhaps I should also note that, if the primary function of a library
is to support research into the farthest depths of obscurity (which may
be important), then the question of size becomes irrelevant.

It is commonly said that a good library has the material that will satisfy the requirements of the user, while a really great library has both those materials and everything else as well. Great libraries are not the concern of this paper. Good libraries are.

With those prefatory remarks, I propose to question here the notion that an academic library must be large in order to be good. It is generally accepted that in any library a large proportion of books circulate infrequently, if at all. Over time, as a library becomes larger and larger, the percentage of little or never used books also becomes larger and larger. So a question arises of optimal collection size, which is in turn a function of the library's purpose. In this paper I want to demonstrate that the optimal size of a library's collections can be stated as a function of recorded circulation demand.

These remarks are meant as prologue to the questions, How large or how small should a library be, and What monographs should make up its collection? (Unless otherwise stated, all comments refer to monographs.)

First, I will review some previous work in the analysis of circulation demand, some of which is very recent, and will then discuss its implication for the general question of collection size.

Some of the library's characteristics are much like those of an industry, although the library is not typically required to show a profit. But there is currently some interest in developing performance standards for libraries that will at least equal in objectivity the use of profit as a measure of success in industry. Circulation analysis can be a major step in that direction.

Let us now consider inventory as a feature common to both industry and libraries. We all know that inventory is necessary for most industries to satisfy customer demands. A salient characteristic of such inventory is that approximately 80 percent of warehouse transactions involve only 20 percent of the categories stocked. The rule is sometimes expressed as the 80/20, or 75/25 rule, allowing for a slight margin of variance. (It is only by coincidence that the figures add to 100; one might, for example, discover that 10 percent of stock categories account for 50 percent of the transactions.)

A similar relationship is often found in sales of business products, where approximately 80 percent of the dollar sales involve only 20 percent of the company's product line.

Libraries exhibit similar relationships. In Figure 1, for example, which correlates titles and circulation transactions for 497 medical journals published from January 1959 through June 1962, we find

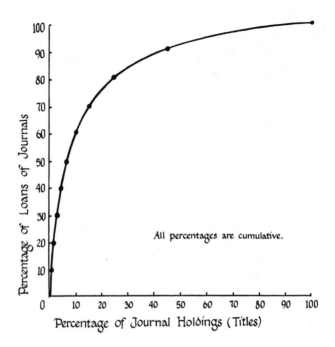

FIGURE 1.   Percentage of loans of medical journals vs. percentage of journal holdings.

that 28 percent of the journal titles accounted for 80 percent of the loans. The curve also depicts the full spectrum of percentage of journal titles required to satisfy a given percentage of circulation demand.

Figure 2 is a plot of the percentage of monograph circulation satisfied versus the percentage of holdings required to satisfy it at the Air Force Cambridge Research Laboratory (AFCRL) Library at Bedford, Massachusetts. Here we note that approximately 80 percent of the circulation requirements are satisfied by approximately 20 percent of the library's holdings. In the same library, about 93 percent of the circulation is satisfied by approximately 50 percent of the holdings.

Figure 2 was developed from the data found in Figure 3. Here in Figure 3 the last (i.e., previous to the current) circulation date was recorded for all books circulated during a six-day period. A cumulative-frequency distribution was then prepared to obtain the

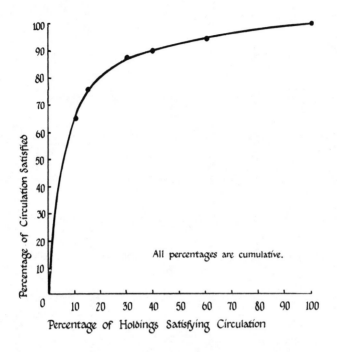

FIGURE 2. Percentage of circulation satisfied vs. percentage of holdings satisfying circulation (AFCRL Library).

plot of percentage of current circulation having previously circulated within time "T". For example, approximately 75 percent of the current circulation has previously circulated at least once within the last twelve months; i.e., each book in this category has a previous circulation date within twelve months. A similar curve prepared from a sampling of the books in the stacks will also be found in Figure 3. We can see that only 15 percent of the books in the stack sample had circulated in the last twelve months, i.e., had a last circulation date within twelve months.

From the foregoing (at the twelve-month point), we can make the statement that approximately *75 percent* of the circulation came from about *15 percent* of the stack holdings. This gives us one point to plot in developing the curve of Figure 2. Another point could be taken from the curves in Figure 3 at time equals thirty-six months. Here we find 87 percent of the circulation coming from, or being satisfied by, 40 percent of the task holdings.

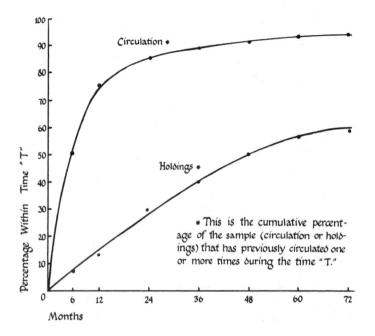

FIGURE 3. Percentage within time "T" vs. time "T" (AFCRL Library).

The curve thus plotted in Figure 2 provides a comprehensive view of that portion of circulation being satisfied by a given portion of stack holdings. Such data could be very useful for developing operating policies and procedures.

The curves in Figures 2 and 3 used limited amounts of data for the library described. However, another study by the author yielded comparable results with a much larger sample from two university libraries. More on this later.

Another operating characteristic curve is plotted in Figure 4, this time for the Forbes Public Library of Northampton, Massachusetts. Again we find that 80 percent of circulation is satisfied by 20 percent of holdings. Figure 4 also provides comprehensive data on the percentage of holdings required to satisfy a given percentage of circulation. For example, 60 percent of the holdings satisfies 99 percent of circulation demand.

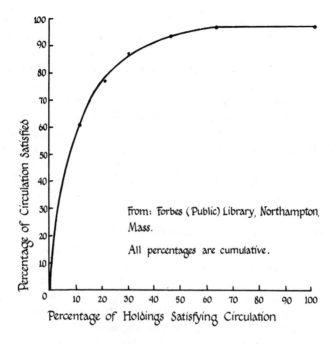

*FIGURE 4. Percentage of circulation satisfied vs. percentage
of holdings satisfying circulation.*

The curves, although from different types of libraries, confirm
quantitatively what is expected intuitively. Using a cumulative-distri-
bution function to present data is quite helpful in understanding
more about the behavioral characteristics of the library user.

The data may also be used to identify holdings to be placed in core
collections. For example, Figures 2 and 3 show that a core collection satisfying approximately 90 percent of the circulation requirements for the AFCRL Library would contain about 50 percent of the
present stack holdings and would consist of all books that circulated
one or more times in the last four years. Similarly, from Figure 4 one
could identify a core collection satisfying 99 percent of the circulation requirements for the Forbes Library, made up of about 60
percent of the present stack holdings. Although not specifically shown
in these data, the criterion of *at least* one circulation in the previous
twelve years would identify those books necessary to satisfy 99 percent of circulation demand.

For the sake of convenience, although it is called the last circulation date (LCD),* the date that is treated as LCD if the book has never circulated is the copyright or accession date of the book. One or the other of these dates has always been recorded as the LCD in the absence of a stamped due date.

The similarities of book circulation and business-inventory holdings are interesting for the sake of knowledge, and revealing in that some techniques of inventory management are readily applicable to libraries. The approach discussed here can be used for stack thinning, core-collection development, multiple-copy determination, and determination of the optimal size of a library's holdings. Its use would, of course, depend upon the library's intended purpose or role.

Regional Libraries and No-Growth Libraries

Data on circulation satisfaction can also be used to make a case for developing substantial interlibrary or regional library centers, particularly for universities and colleges. These would be partially automated and possibly computer-controlled, readily retrievable collections of lesser used material. Smaller core collections of high-demand titles would be available at libraries belonging to the cooperative. The size of the core collections would be calculated to fulfill some specified level of circulation demand, such as 99 percent.

Such a regional system would also provide that any item requested from the lesser used area will automatically re-enter the core collection. Thus, the core collection would continue to meet user-circulation requirements regardless of the source of the items. It appears possible to employ such a system to reduce current requirements for larger and larger libraries to hold larger and larger collections.

Circulation Satisfaction and Stack Thinning

Certain preliminary comments must be made about stack thinning and weeding to put the subject in proper perspective. There has been much debate about the merits of stack thinning or weeding. Weeding creates the problem of a user needing books that have been

---

*Note that throughout this paper, when the term "LCD" is used in speaking of books *that have just returned from circulation,* it should always be understood to refer to the last circulation date *previous to* the current loan. When applied to books that are inspected while they are in the stacks, the term means exactly what it says: the last circulation date stamped in the book.

removed and possibly discarded from the library's holdings. Conversely, if all books are held, even when the chance of use is remote, operating costs must increase as long as the library grows.

I should emphasize, therefore, that I do not advocate full-scale thinning of any library, even by the method described in this paper, until library administrators have accurately weighed its potential effects on library cost, goals, and responsibilities to the user. I am describing a technique that has substantial value as a guide to stack thinning and multiple-copy acquisition; but the decision to weed and subsequently store or discard the weeded volumes is a policy decision. It must be made by library administrators, based on the overall objectives of the library and the needs of its users. A limited access storage area or a regional library are possible alternatives to outright discarding or complete retention.

The data presented here may be of value to librarians in improving service by increasing the probability that users will find what they want. This can be done by analytically predicting multiple-copy needs. It may also be possible to optimize the size of holdings, with respect to measurable user requirements, in those libraries where operating policy and objectives permit or require such an approach. The university library, for example, may be forced by its very nature as a research library to maintain all holdings on campus but to separate them into a low-use storage area and a high-use core area.

A major problem confronting librarians today is how to cope with rapidly growing collections. The continuing stream of incoming books must be offset by a comparable outflow of books that are no longer needed by the library, or holdings will increase at a rate equal to the difference of these two flows. Many libraries have found it necessary to construct additions, and in some cases entirely new libraries, to cope with this and other problems relating to space. Others are attempting to hold the line by thinning stacks of books no longer in high demand.

The usual approach to stack thinning is to have a professional staff member examine books to make a decision based on recorded use of the book, age, subject area, title, author, and many other factors, both qualitative and quantitative, with the end result being somewhat subjective. This end result is sometimes of questionable value because the librarian is not always sufficiently familiar with the subject field to make a correct determination of the book's potential value. Some books are kept that are not really needed, and some books that should not be removed are discarded or are taken to a remote storage area. The extent of these errors in thinning is not always fully appreciated. Weeding decisions made by faculty experts are usually even less reliable than those made by librarians. Subject expertise counts for very little when the central problem is to predict mass behavior of a very large population of library users.

The approach described here centers on the basic imperative of satisfying measurable circulation demand. It is realized that there are other reasons for keeping certain rarely, if ever, used monographs. The proper scale for such rarely used and special collection items is, as previously stated, a library policy decision and will not be considered here.

It is generally agreed that the primary purpose of a library is to supply the information and, in particular, the books required by the user when the user wants them. However, several studies show that there is approximately a fifty-fifty chance (actual probability found was 0.40 to 0.45) of the user not finding the book he wants in the stacks, given that the book is part of the library's holdings. Such a disappointment rate is rather large for a system designed to provide books for its users. Such a performance would not be tolerated in industrial inventory control. The problem can be solved by providing duplicate copies. One must then determine which books should have duplicate copies, and how many. There is also the question of whether there should be a noncirculating core collection.

Kilgour (1961), and later Trueswell (1964), approached the description of user circulation requirements through the statistic of age of the volume. This statistic, when translated into a percentage of holdings satisfying a given percentage of circulation, does not lend itself to thinning of monographs. It does, however, have possibilities for journals. Later studies by Kilgour (1962, 1964) show very high use of a small percentage of medical journals in the Yale Medical Library. For example, 37 of the 1,437 journals received furnished 49 percent of the recorded use.

Basic Approach

As an approach to the problems described above, the last circulation date for books currently being charged was considered to be indicative of the future use of the book. Table 1 is a cumulative distribution of this statistic for a sample taken from the circulation of the Deering Library at Northwestern University. It is generally accepted

Table 1. Deering Library Circulation Previous Charge Date

TIME PERIOD IN MONTHS PRIOR TO CIRCULATION DATE OF SAMPLE	% OF SAMPLE NOT PREVIOUSLY CHARGED OUT DURING THE CUMULATIVE TIME PERIOD
0	100%
1	89
2	76
3	68
4	59
5	51
6	49
7	42
8	39
9	38
10	35
11	32
12	29
18	24
24	17
36	11
48	8.2
60	5.8
Prior to 60th month	0

that certain books are used more frequently than others, which would lead one to expect that in any day's circulation there will be more books that have been previously charged within the last few months and fewer books that have been previously charged one or more years prior to this current circulation date. Thus, we find that of a sample of current circulation, 11 percent was made up of extremely popular books that had been charged out at least once during the previous month. Similarly, 41 percent of the current sample had been charged out at least once during the previous four-month period.

Figure 5 is a plot of the same information and is, in effect, a distribution of the current circulation sample with respect to the previous loan date for each book. It shows the percentage of the sample that had *not* previously circulated. (It has been suggested [Trueswell, 1964] that this information could be used to deveop a relatively low-cost method for converting the library's manual circulation control system to a punched card or computerized circulation control system.) Again, as an illustration, approximately 30 percent of the current circulation sample was made up of books that had not been

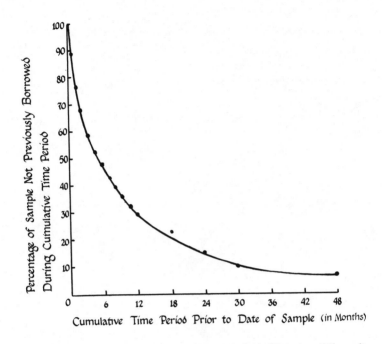

FIGURE 5.   Last circulation date analysis (Deering Library).

previously charged during the past twelve months. Similarly, about 8 percent had not been charged in the past forty-eight months.

Table 2 and Figure 6 represent similar data for the Technological Institute of Northwestern University. Here we find that in only 3 percent of the circulation sample did the last charge date occur sometime prior to the last thirty-six months.

These statistics can be expressed in another way; namely, to say, in the case of the Tech Library, that 97 percent of the current circulation is made up of books that have been charged one or more times during the previous thirty-six months. Thus, if the library holdings were to contain only those books that had been previously charged during the last thirty-six months, one could then expect to satisfy 97 percent of the current circulation requirements (leaving 3 percent to be filled via interloan, and other methods). The actual distribution of the samples taken at the Technological Institute Library and the Deering Library went back further than thirty-six months, and a less-than-1 percent level of nonsatisfaction could be determined for

Table 2. Tech Library Circulation Previous Charge Date

TIME PERIOD IN MONTHS PRIOR TO CIRCULATION DATE OF SAMPLE	% OF SAMPLE NOT PREVIOUSLY CHARGED OUT DURING THE CUMULATIVE TIME PERIOD
0	100%
1	79
2	49
3	42
4	34
5	26
6	25
7	23
8	19
9	17
10	16
11	13
12	12
13	12
14	11
15	11
16	10
17	10
18	9
19	8
20	8
21	7
22	7
23	6
24	6
36	3
Prior to 36th month	0

each of these libraries. In the case of the Technological Institute Library, the over-99 percent figure for circulation satisfaction was comprised of books having LCD within the past eight years. For the Deering Library, it was found that the over-99 percent point was represented by books that had circulated at least once during the past twenty years.

Thus, we might also conclude that 99 percent of current circulation will consist of books (in the case of the Tech Library) that circulated at least once during the previous eight-year period. We now have a way to remove books from the stacks by using the following decision rule: remove all books that have not circulated during the previous

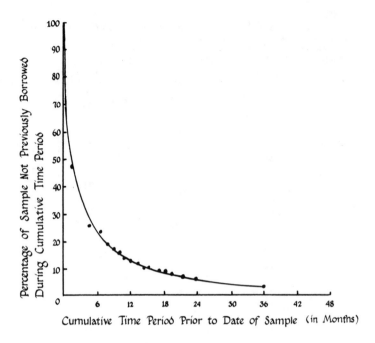

FIGURE 6.   Last circulation date analysis (Tech Library).

eight-year period. Then, we would expect that no more than 1 percent of the users' circulation demand would not be satisfied.

The question that next presents itself is, if such a decision rule is put
into effect, how many books will be removed from the library and
what will be the size of the resulting "optimal" core collection? This
figure can be predicted by again examining Figures 5 and 6. If we use
the eight-year period for the Technological Institute which provides
for 99-percent satisfaction of user requirements, we can simulate or
"build" a hypothetical collection of books based on the circulation
that has occurred during the eight-year period.

If we make the rather loose assumption that the circulation pattern
obtained from the current circulation sample is roughly equivalent to
the circulation patterns for each of the past eight years (some evidence
has been uncovered that supports this assumption), we can attempt to
predict the size of the 99 percent core collection. For example, if we
start eight years back in time and consider the first month of circulation, we will find that 100 percent of the books circulated during this

first month would not have previously circulated since the beginning of this eight-year period (i.e., during the first month). Similarly, from Figure 6 after six months of circulation, approximately 25 percent of these books (current circulation) would not have previously circulated (i.e., during the first six months).

Thus, as each month goes by, we find a certain quantity of books that have not previously circulated since the beginning of the point in time eight years past. Therefore, using circulation figures over the eight-year time period, we can estimate the size of this 99 percent core collection (e.g., books that have circulated one or more times in the eight-year period) by multiplying the percentage of the current circulation that has not previously circulated (since the beginning of the eight-year period) by the circulation for each successive month of the eight-year period. As time progresses, in fact after thirty-six months, we find from Figure 6 that only about 3 percent of the books currently being circulated have not previously circulated since the beginning of the eight-year period. If this calculation is continued, that is, for each month after the eight-year point in time, we can then compute or estimate the size of the core collection (i.e., those books having circulated one or more times during the past eight years).

This calculation was made for the Deering Library and for the Technological Institute Library at Northwestern, and it was found that approximately 25 percent of the current holdings of the Tech Library should satisfy over 99 percent of the current circulation requirements. Similarly, a figure of about 40 percent was obtained for the Deering Library. More will follow about an attempt to validate these percentages.

In summary, this approach centers around the use of the cumulative distribution function of the previous circulation date. Assuming that this distribution function represents typical circulation for the given library, the 99 percentile position is then determined, and this point in time is considered to be the cutting point for thinning the stacks. Such a cutting point should, if the system works properly, provide a collection that will satisfy over 99 percent of the current circulation requirements. If the resulting distribution and previous monthly circulation figures are then multiplied together for each of the corresponding months since the point in time established by the 99 percentile point, one can then calculate the expected size of the core collection. According to the very limited data and small samples taken at the Technological Institute Library and the Deering Library, it was predicted that such core collections satisfying over 99 percent of the circulation requirements at each of these libraries would consist of books that represented approximately 25 percent and 40 percent of the present holdings. Thus, it is inferred that 60 to 70 percent of the holdings might be removed to temporary storage, to an interlibrary center, or to another limited access area.

Certain very questionable assumptions were made in the above approach. The major assumption is that the cumulative distribution function for the current circulation was descriptive of circulation over time during the life of the library, or at least back to the 99 percentile position. Such an assumption seems reasonable, but cannot be accepted as valid without information taken over time for the libraries concerned. However, if the cumulative distribution correctly represents the circulation requirements of the users and if this distribution is typical over time, then the approach is reasonable.

It should be noted that no attempt has been made to evaluate the effect of this approach on in-stack use or browsing. Herman Fussler concluded that, generally, those types of books with high circulation use also had high in-stack use. These relationships should be explored further. There is also the question of the value of the given volume to the user. The needs of a research scientist working on an urgent problem of national importance certainly exceed the needs of a freshman doing a homework problem. This study has, by its very design, assumed equal values in both of these situations. It would be possible, however, to categorize the users and develop user-differentiated, cumulative distribution functions and then to apply these to operating policies. See Trueswell (1970) for a discussion of one aspect of this problem.

Evaluation of Method

In an attempt to evaluate this technique in actual practice, an analysis was made of a one-week circulation sample in the 820s and 830s of the Deering Library. In both of these areas, the less-than-1 percent point occurred at the thirteen-year mark. Summing the products of monthly circulation and the percentage not previously circulated since the thirteen-year period began, it was possible to calculate or predict a core collection size that should satisfy over 99 percent of current circulation requirements. In the case of the 820s, it was predicted that such a core collection would contain 26,428 volumes, or 82.6 percent of the present holdings. Similar computations for the

830s predicted the core collection at approximately 54.2 percent of the present stack holdings.

As a test of the validity of this approach, a 2.7-percent random sample of those books in the stacks in the 820s and 830s was made and the last circulation date recorded. The decision rule was then applied that books would be removed from the collection if LCD occurred prior to the past thirteen years. Application of this decision rule to the stack sample provided a sample core collection of 79.6 percent and 54 percent for the 820s and 830s. These values can now be compared to the predicted values of 82.6 percent and 54.2 percent. While the extreme closeness of these two sets of figures arrived at by two different methods is partly a result of chance, it does indicate a very strong possibility that the technique is valid.

Multiple Copies and/or Noncirculating Copies

The same method can be used for thinning stacks and for determining the requirements for multiple copies or noncirculating copies. The need for multiple or noncirculating copies could be predicted or determined by considering the cumulative frequency distribution of LCD for current circulation and by pre-defining or pre-deciding the percentage of current circulation requirements to be satisfied by a noncirculating or multicopy core collection. Thus, it might be decided as a policy statement that a noncirculating core collection would be such that it would satisfy 90 percent of the circulation requirements. Examination of Figure 2 indicates that the criterion for identifying volumes necessary to yield 90 percent satisfaction would be an LCD within the past eighteen months. By calculations already described, the size of this collection could also be predicted.

Data Collection for LCD

The following are details of the procedures used to collect data. The book cards for each day's circulation were saved, and the last previous circulation date for each was recorded with subsequent punching in tabulating cards. The first three digits of the class number were also recorded and subsequently punched. The latter information permitted analyses within subject areas and also an analysis by "age" of the book (that is, the age or the time since the book entered the library and received an accession number). These cards were then sorted by the last previous circulation date and were listed on an accounting machine. Using this printout, it was possible to locate the 99 percentile as well as group by monthly and yearly intervals. This information was then plotted as shown earlier in Figures 5 and 6. In the few cases where the current circulation date was the only entry on the book card, some interpretation was necessary because this could indicate either a new book card (replacing a used-up one) or a first circulation. Most of these cases could be resolved by comparing the age of the book from the accession number with the apparent age of the card from its physical appearance.

The last circulation date for books in the stacks (820s and 830s) was determined by physical examination of the book card in the pocket of the book. The sampling procedure used was to take the second book from each shelf in the stacks for the subject area sampled. This provided a 2.7-percent sample of the books. There is some question as to whether this sample is truly random, considering the fact that the books are placed within subject categories when the Dewey Decimal classification system is used. Further research on sampling procedures is needed. The information taken from book cards of books in the stacks was then examined to determine the number of volumes that have their LCD on or before the 99 percentile date for the circulated books. Knowing the number of volumes in the sample, it was then possible to determine the percentage of holdings that had an LCD older than the one specified. This percentage indicates the proportion of the stack holdings that would be removed if the 99 percentile date (predicted from circulation requirements) were used to thin the holdings.

Comparisons Between Libraries

Comments made so far deal with analyses of limited data from portions of a given library and relate to a specific library at a specific time. Since then, substantial amounts of data have been collected at the libraries of the University of Massachusetts, Mount Holyoke College, and Forbes Public Library. Each of these three libraries was studied in considerable detail, and rather extensive samples of data were taken and analyzed. The following is a brief discussion of some of the results of this data-taking.

The first example for comparative purposes was taken from the very limited stack sample data of the Deering Library of Northwestern Library, specifically the 820s. Figure 7 is a cumulative distribution

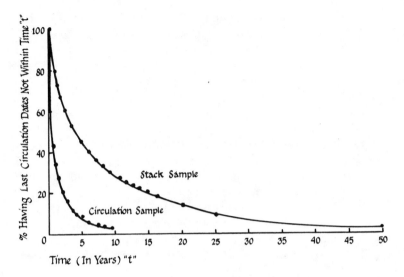

FIGURE 7.   Circulation and stack samples (Deering Library, 820s).

function representing a sampling of circulation and of stack holdings. It should be noted that the plot of the circulation sample described the circulation according to the LCD parameter. As previously noted, the plot reveals the percentage of monographs having LCD not within the time period indicated, i.e., the percentage of current circulation not previously circulated within time "T." For example, only about 7 percent of the circulation sample had not previously circulated during the past five years. The stack sample curve represents comparable data taken from a sampling of the books in the stacks (820s).

Using both curves in Figure 7, it is possible to make such remarks as the following: at the five-year mark on the plot, approximately 7 percent of the circulation sample had LCD not within five years, or in effect were taken from a subset or portion of the stack population that comprised approximately 40 percent of the stack holdings. Expressed differently, 93 percent of the circulation came from 60 percent of the holdings. As a second example, at the two-year LCD mark the statement could be made that 20 percent of the stack holdings satisfied approximately 70 percent of the current circulation sample.

From the information provided in Figure 7, it is possible to make statements about that portion of current circulation that is satisfied by a given percent of stack holdings. Figure 8 represents a combining of the two curves found on Figure 7. Thus, we have determined points on the curve in Figure 8 referring to their corresponding values on the stack sample curve and the circulation sample curve in Figure 7 for a given time period. For example, in Figure 8 we see that approximately 50 percent of the holdings satisfy 90 percent of the circulation requirements.

The data in Figures 7 and 8 represent a very small portion or subset of the holdings at the Deering Library at Northwestern University. A greater quantity of data has been collected at the Goodell Library of the University of Massachusetts and at the library of Mount Holyoke College. The study at the Goodell Library covered one and one half months and approximately 5,000 circulation transactions. These circulation data are plotted on Figure 9, along with stack holdings data, and provide some comparison with the very limited data from Northwestern University. Note that for simplicity the plots are now labeled LCD "within" the time period rather than "not within." Here, for ex-

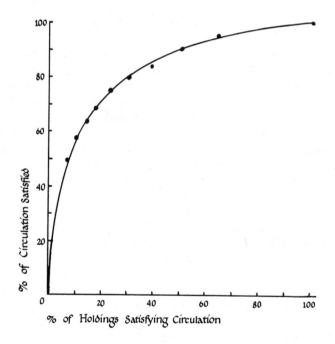

FIGURE 8.   Percentage of circulation satisfied vs. percentage of holdings from which circulation taken (Deering Library, 820s).

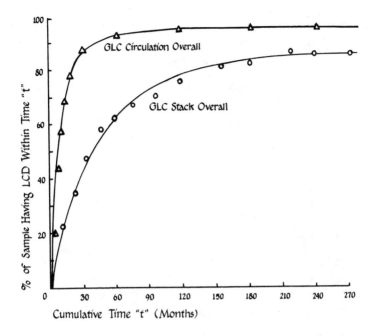

FIGURE 9.   Circulation and stack samples overall (Goodell Library).

ample, 50 percent of the holdings satisfy approximately 90 percent of the circulation requirements. Figure 10 shows an operating characteristic curve similar to Figure 8 but applying to the University of Massachusetts. The UMass stack sample was approximately one-half of 1 percent of the library's holdings. The sampling procedure leaves some question as to the randomness of the sample because selection was made from a fixed number of shelves and a fixed indentation on each shelf.

Figures 11 and 12 contain a plot of LCD for the Mount Holyoke College library circulation as recorded over a four-month period. Approximately 9,000 transactions were recorded in this sample. Also plotted on Figure 11 for comparison is the LCD information for the circulation sample from the Goodell Library and from the Deering Library at Northwestern University (over a relatively short period of about one or two weeks).

It is interesting to note the similarity of these plots, as they represent the experiences of three different libraries with widely vary-

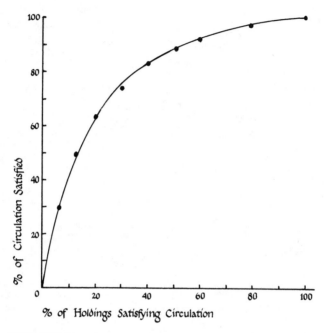

FIGURE 10.   Percentage of circulation satisfied vs. percentage of holdings from which circulation taken (Goodell Library,
stack and circulation data).

ing collection size. The shape of the curves indicates that a small
number of books at each library circulate very frequently, and suggests that these books could comprise a core collection.

The stack sample at the Mount Holyoke library was also taken during the summer months when circulation was at a minimum. These
data (approximately 1 percent of the holdings) were then plotted as
shown in Figure 12. The stack sample data were then plotted against
the circulation sample data to obtain the plot shown in Figure 13,
entitled "Percentage circulation satisfied vs. percentage holdings
from which circulation taken." This curve is similar to Figures 8 and
10 and illustrates the percentage of the holdings satisfying a given percentage of circulation. For example, we note from Figure 13 that
approximately 85 percent of the circulation is satisfied by 40 percent
of the holdings. These data are quite different from the data collected
for the 820s at Northwestern University. The 820s data were taken
from a relatively small sample of a narrow subject category.

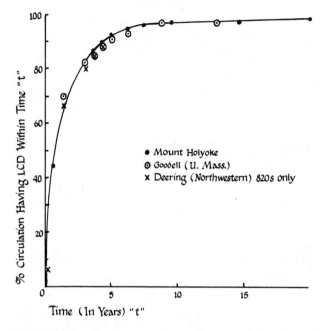

FIGURE 11.   Percentage of circulation within time "t."

Figures 10 and 13 show that the operating characteristics for the University of Massachusetts library and Mount Holyoke College library are rather similar.

Using this kind of information, it is now possible to define core collections to meet any desired percentage of circulation satisfaction. For example, in Figure 13 we could define a core collection comprised of approximately 60 percent of the current holdings that would satisfy over 94 percent of current circulation requirements. Such a core collection could be identified by its LCD as taken from Figures 9 and 10. We have now reviewed in a limited manner some additional research on LCD as a parameter for describing library circulation patterns. Based on over 15,000 library transactions, this more recent research indicates that the circulation pattern of a given library when described by using a cumulative distribution function of the LCD may be similar, if not identical, to those found at other libraries. When correlated with similar distributions of stack holdings, it is possible to define and identify core collections that will satisfy a given percentage of circulation requirements.

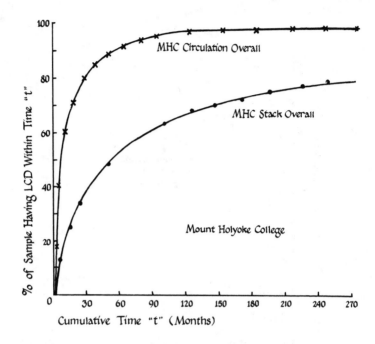

FIGURE 12.   Circulation and stack samples overall (Mount Holyoke College).

As we have shown from the above research, there are definite similarities between the operating characteristic curves for Mount Holyoke, the University of Massachusetts, and the limited data taken from the Northwestern Deering Library. Additional data have been collected by S. Slote from a number of public libraries in New Jersey. Slote's data have been analyzed, and operating characteristics have been developed for each of the public libraries. These are plotted in Figure 14 along with the data from Mount Holyoke, the University of Massachusetts, and the limited data from Northwestern's Deering Library. It is quite interesting to see the similarity between the operating characteristics for these libraries. As discussed earlier, it is particularly of interest to find that the distribution of LCD for circulation data was very similar for the college libraries.

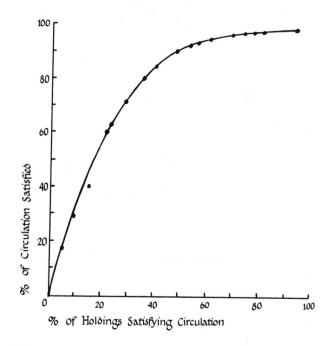

FIGURE 13.   Percentage of circulation satisfied vs. percentage of holdings from which circulation taken (Mount Holyoke College, stack and circulation data).

LCD Distribution Changes Over Time

During much of the discussion of the LCD distribution for circulation data, the assumption has been made that the distribution does not change over time. Given the patterns of similarity between libraries and the general nature of the data, this seems to be a reasonable assumption. However, assumptions are made to be checked and, therefore, some additional data (not previously published) have been collected by Trueswell and Tyma.

The University of Massachusetts Library was chosen for the study because of its convenience and availability. Data were collected on 6,087 monograph circulation transactions during the period March 17-23, 1974. The data were then analyzed, and cumulative distribution functions were developed for each of the subcategories of the

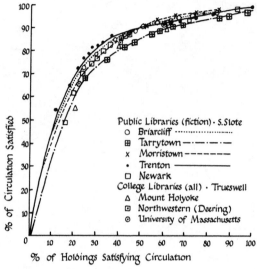

Note: To avoid congestion, only four curves are drawn.

FIGURE 14

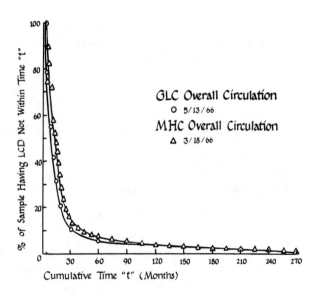

FIGURE 15

Dewey Decimal System. It was necessary to convert the present LC categories to the Dewey System because the original 1968 report by Trueswell used the Dewey System as the base.

The cumulative distribution functions for the LCD for circulation data in 1974 were superimposed on the plots prepared from the 1966 data as published in 1968. Approximately eight years passed between the two points of data-taking. During this eight-year period, the University of Massachusetts Library moved into an entirely new building and the student body increased in size considerably, resulting in an increased quantity of circulation. Circulation increased from 113,199 per year in 1966 to 235,296 per year in 1973. However, the LCD distribution has remained essentially the same.

As an aside, Figure 15 is a plot of the 1966 data for Mount Holyoke College compared to the 1966 data for the University of Massachusetts. As stated previously, these distributions are quite similar. Figure 16 is a plot of the 1974 data superimposed on the original plot of the 1966 data. Here again, the similarities of the two distributions are quite apparent. Figure 17 is a plot of the 1974 UMass data superimposed on the comparable plot for 1966 data using Dewey class 100 to 299. Figure 18 is a similar plot for the 300s of the Dewey System, and Figure 19 is a plot for the 900s.

Thus, we have been able to show earlier that data collected at different libraries have shown marked similarities between the distributions of LCD for circulation. Furthermore, data taken between two time datum points, eight years apart, also show marked similarity for the same library.

During the summer of 1974, an attempt was made to replicate the 1966 stack sample data. A stack sample of approximately 2,700 books was taken from the UMass library.

Figure 20 is a plot of the 1974 stack data superimposed on the 1966 data. The similarities found in the circulation data are obviously not repeated in the stack data. However, analysis of the phenomenon of the stack distribution shows that this might be expected. During the nine years that have passed since the original data were taken, a rather large number of books have been acquired in the library, and many of these have not circulated. As a result, the curve of the stack sample as shown in Figure 20 has been displaced upward. This results in a somewhat modified operating characteristic curve as shown in Figure 21. Here again, the change from the 1966 operating characteristic to the 1974 operating characteristic is expected as it reflects the

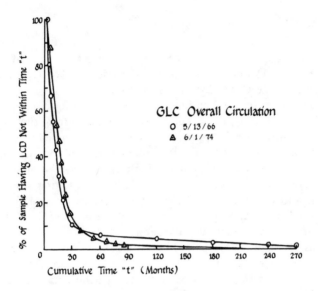

FIGURE 16

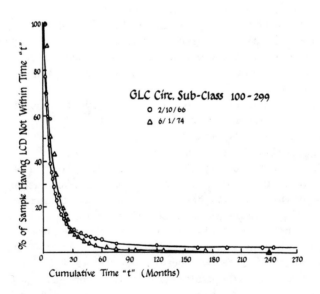

FIGURE 17

increased holdings of the library. This effectively makes for an operating characteristic shifted away from the diagonal.

Ideally, one would like to have the operating characteristic shifted toward the diagonal because, theoretically, this represents the perhaps desirable state of affairs where the holdings are more uniform in their satisfaction of circulation. The operating characteristic for the 1974 data (UMass) has shifted away from the diagonal, indicating a larger number of lesser used books. This, in effect, places proportionally greater circulation demand on a given portion of the stack holdings.

In 1966 we found that 20 percent of the holdings satisfied 66 percent of the circulation; yet, in 1974, 20 percent of the holdings satisfied 80 percent of the circulation. This kind of information can be useful, but it also shows a situation in 1974 which can be considered as less desirable because a greater proportion of the circulation is taken from the same portion of the holdings. Thus, one might infer that this uneven distribution or allocation of circulation demand across the

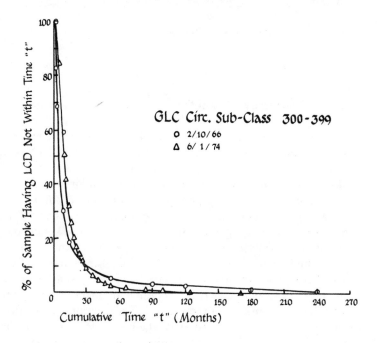

FIGURE 18

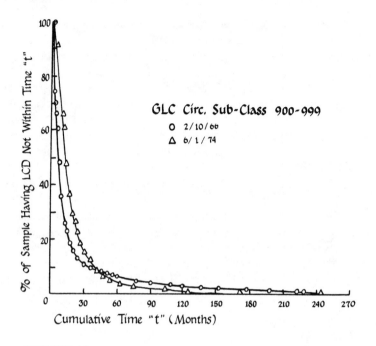

FIGURE 19

holdings of the library is less optimal, i.e., the holdings are not being used uniformly. More research should be done on this subject.

Perhaps an even more significant conclusion can be reached from this kind of analysis; namely, that when we speak of satisfying a given percentage of circulation demand, we are speaking of the number of books that have circulated one or more times in a given number of years. This quantity of books appears to be a function only of the LCD circulation distribution and the rate of circulation (i.e., when defined at the given percentage of circulation satisfied). The LCD circulation distribution appears to be practically the same for most college libraries, and circulation is usually a function of the number of students allowed to use the library. Perhaps then, for a given percentage of circulation satisfaction there is an optimal number of holdings and this number is a function of the amount of circulation; or, in effect, the number of students allowed to use the library. A corollary is that there may be a core collection that satisfies a given percentage of circulation demand, say 99 percent, and that the optimal size of this core

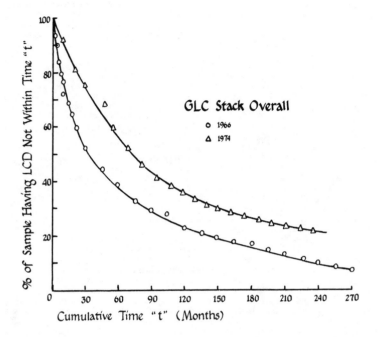

FIGURE 20

is arithmetically related to the size of the student body. More research needs to be done on this also.

Mathematical Formula

A formula was developed (by S. Turner, one of my doctoral students) for the purpose of mathematically expressing the LCD distributions for circulation and for stack holdings, where P is the proportion of books having LCD not within time "t."

$$P = \left(\frac{a}{t+a} \right)^b$$

where $a \geq 0$ and $b \geq 0$.

This formula was plotted on Figure 22 for circulation data. Note that it approximates the data quite well. Figure 23 is a plot for stack holdings. The plots in both of these figures are superimposed on the 1966 data.

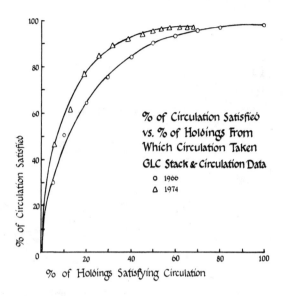

FIGURE 21

Conclusion

In the no-growth collection new books must still be added, but little-used books will be removed at a comparable rate. Savings will occur not in limited-access storage for one library but in cooperative library centers containing the little-used books from several libraries. There is some evidence that essentially the same titles will be found among the little-used books of most college libraries. The regional library would simply keep one copy of each title, discarding the rest, and thus greatly reduce aggregate storage costs of the participating libraries.

For any kind of measurement and control of circulation demand, circulation records must be maintained. It appears that the easiest record to use is the LCD, and therefore an appeal is made that librarians maintain procedures that insure date stamping of the book itself.

Although the use of the LCD distribution is not the total answer to space problems, it is a reliable tool for developing optimally sized holdings, as based on one or more stated criteria of library policies and objectives.

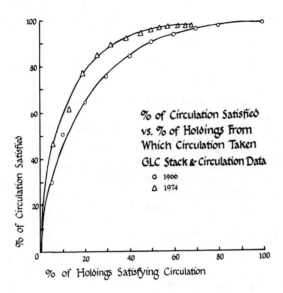

FIGURE 22

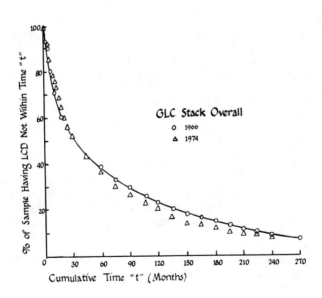

FIGURE 23

Bibliography

FUSSLER, HERMAN H., and SIMON, J. L. *Patterns in the Use of Books in Large Research Libraries.* Chicago: University of Chicago Library, 1961.

KILGOUR, F. G. "Recorded Use of Books in the Yale Medical Library." *American Documentation* 12 (October 1961): 266-269.

———. "Use of Medical and Biological Journals in the Yale Medical Library." *Bulletin of the Medical Library Association* 50, no. 3 (July 1962): 429-449.

HAMBURG, MORRIS, CLELLAND, RICHARD C., BOMMER,. MICHAEL R. W., RAMIST, LEONARD E., and WHITFIELD, RONALD M. *Library Planning and Decision-making Systems.* Cambridge, Mass: MIT Press, 1974.

MCGRATH, WILLIAM E. "Correlating the Subjects of Books Taken Out of and Books Used Within an Open-stack Library." *College and Research Libraries* 32 (1971): 280-285.

TRUESWELL, RICHARD W. "User Behavioral Patterns and Requirements and Their Effect on the Possible Applications of Data Processing and Computer Techniques in a University Library." Northwestern University, Ph.D. Dissertation, 1964.

———. "Two Characteristics of Circulation and Their Effect on the Implementation of Mechanized Circulation Control Systems." *College and Research Libraries* (July 1964): 285-291.

———. "Determining the Optimal Number of Volumes for a Library's Holdings." Paper presented at the joint meeting of Operations Research Society of America and the Institute for Management Sciences, Minneapolis, Minnesota, October 7-9, 1964.

———. "A Quantitative Measure of User Circulation Requirements and Its Possible Effect on Stack Thinning and Multiple Copy Determination." *American Documentation* 16 (January 1965): 20-25.

———. "The Library As an Inventory Problem." Paper presented at the 27th National Meeting, Operations Research Society of America, Boston, Massachusetts, May 6-7, 1965.

———. "Determining the Optimal Number of Volumes for a Library's Core Collection." *Libri* 16, no. 1 (1966): 49-60.

———. *Analysis of Library User Circulation Requirements.* Final Report, January 1968, Supported by NSF Grant GN-0435, 108 pp.

———. "Some Circulation Data from a Research Library." *College and Research Libraries* 29, no. 6, (November 1968): 493-95.

———. "User Circulation Satisfaction vs. Size of Holdings at Three Academic Libraries." *College and Research Libraries* 30, no. 3 (May 1969): 204-213.

———. "Some Behavioral Patterns of Library Users, The 80/20 Rule." *Wilson Library Bulletin* 43, no. 5 (January 1969): 458-61.

———. "Article Use and Its Relationship to Individual User Satisfaction." *College and Research Libraries* 31, no. 4 (July 1970): 239-245.

TYMA, MARK S. "Analysis of Library Circulation Data." Term Report, Department of Industrial Engineering and Operations Research, University of Massachusetts at Amherst, June 1974.

Blair Stewart

The Optimum Size for Periodical Collections in Liberal Arts College Libraries

A typical attitude toward periodical collections in the liberal arts library is that bigger is better. This attitude is found not only among librarians, but among faculty members, accrediting organizations, and even college administrators. But surely bigger is better only up to a point, and there must be an optimum size for the periodical collection of a given college library. The college library successful in conducting its periodical acquisition and retention procedures in an informed and rational manner could presumably approximate this optimum.

Many considerations enter into decisions to acquire or dispose of individual periodical titles. A basic assumption made in the following discussion is that such decisions should be based on the extent to which the periodical is read by the library's users. The acceptance of this assumption also implies the proposition that the policies of a liberal arts college library should be designed to provide students and faculty with prompt access to the periodical literature they request, with no financial penalties for requesting periodicals not in its holdings. Prompt access means on-site availability of heavily used journals and efficient interlibrary availability of missing issues—or pages—of heavily used periodicals and of titles so costly or so infrequently consulted that holding them would be excessively expensive per use. The college library should not be expected to serve as a mausoleum in which unused periodicals are interred on the chance that future generations may benefit by exhuming them and examining their bones. It follows, then, that decisions on acquiring and retaining periodicals should be based on the amount of use made of them related to the costs of acquiring and holding them, and the costs and delays in obtaining photocopies of desired articles in them by means of inter-library service.

It should be added that not all uses have equal weight. Instructional and research interests may count for more than recreational reading, and anyone familiar with the culture of a college campus recognizes the impact of the hierarchical structure on the relative importance of requests from different sources. Unfortunately, in this study these differences cannot be taken into account, and all requests for access to periodical literature are treated as though they were of equal importance.

If use is accepted as an appropriate determinant of periodical acquisition and retention policies, we must conclude that the present procedures in most liberal arts college libraries are irrational. Many such libraries penalize readers by levying charges for photocopies from periodicals not in their own holdings. At the same time they spend substantial sums in acquiring and holding periodicals that are never read.

Most college libraries, of course, have very sketchy information on how much their readers make use of each periodical. If use is to be the test of the desirability of acquiring and holding a periodical, it is extremely difficult, if not impossible, to follow defensible policies without such information. Since it is difficult to acquire direct information, librarians have generally relied on indirect indications of use, and have naturally tended to give weight to pressures from administrators, faculty members, and on occasion, students. While these and other means facilitate identification of heavily used periodicals, they do not enable easy identification of periodicals that are used very infrequently or never. It is on these periodicals that much money is being wasted.

Liberal arts college librarians have had the assistance of well-considered advice in identifying periodicals they should have. A program of publishing lists of recommended periodicals for college libraries was begun by G. R. Lyle in 1931-1932 with a list published in the *Wilson Bulletin for Libraries*. This has been followed by the

Classified List of Periodicals for the College Library, by Evan I. Farber, which has now gone through five editions. The basic idea behind Farber's effort is the eminently sensible one that need patterns in different liberal arts college libraries are probably quite similar. It is interesting, therefore, to determine whether the holdings of the ten member libraries of the Periodical Bank of the Associated Colleges of the Midwest are basically similar and to what extent their holdings agree with the latest Farber list.

A study of the periodical holdings (other than bibliographic publications) of these ten liberal arts college libraries revealed that, as of June 1972, their holdings were extremely diverse. These libraries held 4,107 different periodicals, but only 85 periodicals, or 2 percent of the total list, were held by all ten. Only 451 titles, or 11 percent of the total list, were held by six or more.

To what extent do the actual periodical acquisition policies of these ten libraries bear out Evan Farber's identification of the most useful periodicals for a college library? Farber places an asterisk by those titles he considers the most important for the college library. Excluding his recommended 23 bibliographical publications, which were not part of the study of Periodical Bank member library holdings, Farber recommended 344 titles for first purchase. One of the 85 periodicals held by all ten libraries had ceased publication by the time Farber's latest list appeared, so only 84 of the 85 titles held by all ten libraries might have appeared on his list. As shown in Table 1, all 84 of these titles are listed by Farber. There was at least this degree of unanimity on appropriate titles for a college library. It accounted for approximately one-quarter of the titles Farber recommended for first pur-

Table 1. Distribution of Titles on Farber's List, by Number of Member Libraries Holding the Title

Number of Libraries	10	9	8	7	6	5	4	3	2	1	0	TOTAL
Number of Selected Titles	84	56	46	36	26	29	28	12	11	13	3	344
Cumulated Number	84	140	186	222	248	277	305	317	328	341	344	

chase. Majority opinion on the list is indicated by the fact that 248 of his list were held by six or more of the ten libraries. This includes 72 percent of the total list. Three titles on the list were not held by any of the ten member libraries: *Columbia Journal of World Business, Quest* (St. Cloud, Minnesota), and *This Magazine Is about Schools.*

The unanimity on the 84 universally held titles was not quite as great as the discussion above implies. If all ten libraries had been subscribing to these periodicals, the total number of their subscriptions would have been 840. As is seen in Table 2, the actual total number of subscriptions was 827. Thirteen of the potential subscriptions to these periodicals had been dropped. There were 11 of the 84 periodicals to which one or more of the member libraries had dropped their subscriptions, although they maintained backfiles on their shelves. This left only 73 periodicals to which all ten libraries were subscribing in 1972.

The data presented in Table 2 provide additional information about the periodical holdings of the ten member libraries. One significant aspect of this table is the classification of titles by their status at the library holding them. The fact that a library drops a sub-

TABLE 2. Current Subscriptions, Dropped Subscriptions, and Ceased Titles, by Number of Periodical Bank Member Libraries Holding the Title, June 1972

| Number of Libraries Holding Title | Active Periodicals | | | | | Ceased Periodicals | Total Titles | |
	Current Subscriptions Number	Subscriptions Dropped No.	%	Titles No.	Cumulative	Number	Number	Cumulative
10	827	13	1.5	84	84	1	85	85
9	783	27	3.3	90	174	1	91	176
8	636	36	5.4	84	258	5	89	265
7	490	21	4.1	73	331	3	76	341
6	661	59	8.2	120	451	8	128	469
5	568	67	10.6	127	578	18	145	614
4	673	79	10.5	188	766	19	207	821
3	659	142	17.7	267	1033	48	315	1136
2	866	182	17.4	524	1557	100	624	1760
1	1242	755	37.8	1997	3554	350	2347	4107
TOTALS	7405	1381	15.7	3554		553	4107	

scription must reflect its judgment that the periodical is not sufficiently useful to warrant continued subscription. Anyone familiar
with the operations of college libraries knows that decisions to drop
subscriptions are not made lightly. It may be seen from Table 2 that
the proportion of dropped subscriptions rises from 1.5 percent for the
titles held by all ten libraries to 37.8 percent for titles held by only one.
This is one bit of evidence suggesting that the number of libraries subscribing to a periodical is a rough indication of its usefulness. There
were 451 active titles held by six or more of the member libraries. If all
the libraries had been subscribing to these 451 periodicals, the total
number of subscriptions would obviously have been 4,510. Actually,
there were 3,397 current subscriptions, or 75.3 percent of the
potential. The difference of 1,113 subscriptions consisted of 957
cases, or 86 percent of the total, where the title was not held at all, and
156 cases where the subscription had been dropped and backfiles
retained.

One of the significant disclosures in Table 2 is that 1,997 active
titles were held by only one library. This is 56 percent of the total
number of active titles held. The proportion of ceased titles held by
one library is even higher—350 of a total of 553, or 63 percent. The
striking manner in which the numbers of dropped subscriptions and
ceased titles increase as the number of libraries holding the titles
decrease presumably reflects the variety of opinions on the
importance of different periodicals for the liberal arts college library.
It also reflects differences in library policies with respect to backfiles.
Examination of the individual holdings lists makes it clear that some
libraries have followed the policy of eliminating backfiles of dropped
or ceased periodicals in all but very few cases. Other libraries seem to
have retained practically everything. One library had only 17 dropped
periodicals and 16 ceased periodicals in its holdings, while another
had 382 dropped and 267 ceased titles. Although these libraries presumably had weeded their collections when the Periodical Bank was
established, they still held substantial files of ceased periodicals and
titles to which subscriptions had been dropped. There were 1,381 files
of periodicals to which subscriptions had been dropped, and there
were 988 files of the 553 ceased periodicals held. The existence of
these 2,369 files of dropped or ceased titles suggests that further
weeding of these collections would be appropriate.

How many periodicals may be rated as useful on the basis of a
majority vote of the member libraries? The answer is found in the

column in Table 2 showing the cumulative number of active titles. There were 451 such titles held by six or more libraries, and 578 held by five or more, 12.7 and 16.3 percent, respectively, of all the titles held. It perhaps should be repeated at this point that these data do not apply to bibliographical tools such as *The Readers' Guide*, or *Chemical Abstracts*. These are some of the most useful, as well as the most expensive, periodicals on the college library's holdings list. But, since they must be used on site and are therefore not held by the Periodical Bank, our data do not provide any information on their usefulness.

It might be inferred from the analysis so far that the number of libraries subscribing to a periodical is being proposed as a sufficient indication of its importance for any liberal arts college library. There are two reasons for rejecting this inference. The first is surely that there are differences among colleges that result in different, and even occasionally unique, needs for periodicals. It is difficult, however, to believe that these unique needs justify subscriptions to 1,242 different periodicals—the number subscribed to by only one member library.

Another reason is the existence of minority opinions with respect to the periodicals held by the majority. In the case of dropped subscriptions, these are obviously based on the experience of owning the title; in the more numerous cases where the periodicals are missing from holdings lists, these exclusions have presumably been made in favor of other periodicals held by these libraries. It seems worthwhile, therefore, to analyze the Periodical Bank use data to see whether they give us clues as to the relative usefulness of different periodicals for the liberal arts college library.

The diversity in the periodical holdings of the ten liberal arts college libraries leads to the conclusion that either Farber's assumption that the periodical needs of liberal arts college libraries are basically similar is not well founded, or that there is much irrationality in the periodical holdings of the ten libraries. This question could be definitively answered only by a study of actual periodical use at the ten libraries. If Farber is correct, many periodicals in these ten libraries are never used, or are used so infrequently that the cost per use is exorbitant. The available evidence tends to support the hypothesis that the typical college library holds many periodicals that are not used at all or are used very infrequently. The Bradley University library, for example, has made a study of the use of its unbound periodicals. It found that it was subscribing to 410 periodicals that had not been checked out once in four years, and 376 additional periodicals that had been checked out less than ten times in that period of time.

Analysis of the requests filled by the Periodical Bank for its member libraries provides indirect information on the usefulness of different periodicals. (See Appendix for the title list of the 150 most frequently requested periodicals.) Table 3 shows the number of requests for article photocopies for currently published periodicals filled by the Periodical Bank in a three-year period for the member libraries, from periodicals held by one or more of the member libraries. This tabulation excludes requests for photocopies from periodicals not owned by any of the member libraries and requests filled for associate members. In this table, the numbers of requests are classified by whether the periodical requested was on the list of holdings of the requesting library and by the number of libraries holding the periodical. One of the most striking facts shown by the table is that one of the cells into which the data on number of requests have been distributed contains more than one-sixth of all the requests filled. This is the cell in the upper left-hand corner of the table showing the number of requests, 6,010, filled for libraries holding the periodical requested when the title was held by all ten member libraries. A priori this was a most unexpected phenomenon. I have reported elsewhere on the results of the analysis of a random sample of these requests. The major reason for requesting photocopies from periodicals on the library's list of holdings is the existence of gaps in the holdings. Of less importance are issues at the bindery or mutilated. One may suspect that there were some cases in which requests were not adequately monitored at the requesting library. In any event, it seems clear that the 84 active periodicals on the holdings lists of all ten libraries were, by the Periodical Bank use test, the most important group in this method of classifying periodicals held by the member libraries.

A second remarkable fact shown by Table 3 is the pronounced decline in the number of requests filled for subscribing libraries as the number of libraries holding the title decreased. There were 71.55 requests filled per title for periodicals held by all ten libraries and only 0.01 requests per title for titles subscribed to by only one library. These figures tend to reinforce the presumption that the number of libraries subscribing to a title is a useful indication of its value in a liberal arts college library.

It may appear that the data for the average number of requests per title for colleges holding the title overstate the importance of access to

TABLE 3. *Requests from Member Libraries Filled by the Periodical Bank, September 1, 1969 Through June 1972, for Periodicals Held by One or More Member Libraries, by Status of Periodical in Holdings of Requesting Library*

Number of Libraries Holding Title	REQUESTS FILLED							
	For Libraries Holding Title			For Libraries Not Holding Title			For All Member Libraries	
	Number	Per Title	Index I	Number	Per Title	Index II	Total	Per Title
10	6,010	71.55	7.16	0	-	-	6,010	71.5
9	3,574	39.71	4.21	734	8.2	8.2	4,308	47.9
8	1,534	18.26	2.28	699	8.3	4.2	2,233	26.6
7	1,010	13.84	1.98	897	12.3	4.1	1,907	26.1
6	1,185	9.88	1.65	1,882	15.7	3.9	3,067	25.6
5	949	7.47	1.49	2,644	20.8	4.2	3,593	28.3
4	665	3.54	0.88	2,028	10.8	1.8	2,693	14.3
3	621	2.33	0.78	2,363	8.9	1.3	2,984	11.2
2	298	0.57	0.29	2,659	5.07	0.6	2,957	5.6
1	150	0.01	0.01	3,500	1.8	0.2	3,650	1.8
TOTALS	15,996	4.50		17,406	4.9		33,402	9.4

INDEX I: Usefulness of periodical photocopy service to libraries holding titles requested: number of requests per title divided by number of libraries holding title.

INDEX II: Usefulness of periodical photocopy service to libraries not holding title requested: number of requests per title divided by number of libraries not holding title.

the Periodical Bank for an individual library, since the average includes the requests filled for ten libraries at one extreme and the requests filled for only one library at the other. Index I is an attempt to correct for this by dividing the average number of requests per title by the number of libraries holding the title. Although the contrast between the highest and lowest figures is naturally less striking than for the average number of requests per title, it is clear not only that access to the Periodical Bank has been useful to libraries owning the periodical requested, but that the number of libraries holding the periodical suggests the degree of such usefulness.

This phenomenon was totally unexpected when the Periodical Bank was formed. At that time it was agreed that the Periodical Bank would not acquire the periodicals owned by all ten of the member libraries. The list of such periodicals was then assumed to include a substantial number of titles. Fortunately, a union list of the periodical holdings of the member libraries was not available, so no one knew the identity of the periodicals owned by all ten libraries. At the outset the Bank received substantial grants to be used for subscriptions and backfiles, and in the process of building its collection acquired 75 of the most heavily used periodicals among the 85 periodicals owned by all ten member libraries.Classified by number of libraries holding the periodical, this was the most useful group of titles acquired by the Bank, although the list included some infrequently requested titles and excluded some heavily used titles.

The second part of Table 3 deals with the usefulness of the Periodical Bank to the member libraries not owning the title requested. This service, originally assumed to be the Bank's sole service, has been somewhat more significant than supplying photocopies from owned titles. When the requests for photocopies from periodicals not owned by the requesting library are considered—including the 3,199 requests for periodicals not owned by any member library—it turns out that 56 percent of the requests filled were from libraries not holding the title requested.

Index II is an attempt to measure the usefulness per title of access to the Periodical Bank for libraries not holding the title requested. In this case the average number of requests filled is divided by the number of libraries *not* holding the title. By this measure, access to the Bank was most useful, on the average, to the libraries not holding titles held by the other nine libraries. The index drops sharply for periodicals not owned by two libraries and then remains fairly constant for periodicals not held by from two to five libraries. From that point on the index declines quite sharply. Both indexes suggest that the Periodical Bank is most useful for those titles owned by five or more member libraries. Reference back to the cumulative total column of Table 2 indicates that there were 578 active periodicals in these more useful groups.

Up to this point, the data presented have dealt exclusively with the holdings and use of the Periodical Bank by the ten member libraries, all of them serving liberal arts colleges. It may be of interest to look also at some of the information accumulated since the Periodical Bank began serving other types of libraries as associate members, including large universities, community colleges, and public libraries. A number of these libraries are obviously using the Periodical Bank as a last resort after failing to obtain desired photocopies from other sources. It is to be expected, therefore, that requests will not be concentrated on such a small list of periodicals as were the requests from ten liberal arts colleges.

Table 4 presents data on requests received by the Periodical Bank during the three academic years during which the Bank served liberal arts college libraries almost exclusively and for the two subsequent years during which the Bank has been serving a more diverse clientele. The titles are ranked in order by the number of requests received during the respective periods, and the data are presented for modules of 50 titles each. The information given covers the requests received for photocopies for the 900 most frequently requested periodicals in the period covered.

If we look first at the data for the first three years, we see that requests to the Periodical Bank were concentrated on a relatively small number of periodicals. The most popular 50 periodicals accounted for 27.5 percent of the requests received. The top 450 periodicals accounted for 75.2 percent of the requests, and the 900 periodicals tabulated accounted for almost 90 percent of the requests received.

When we turn to the data for the last two years, we discover that the requests for photocopies increased. Hence, the total of requests for the two years is slightly greater than the total for the previous three years, but requests have indeed become dispersed over a much larger number of periodicals. The pattern of concentration on relatively few titles still persists. However, approximately one-half of the requests received were concentrated on 300 titles, but the 900 most heavily used periodicals accounted for only 63 percent of the requests

TABLE 4. *Number of Requests for Periodical Photocopies Received by the Periodical Bank in Three Academic Years, September 1, 1969 to June 30, 1972; and in Two Years, July 1, 1972 to June 30, 1974, in Modules of Fifty Titles in Descending Order of Number of Requests*

Rank of Periodicals	September 1, 1969 to June 30, 1972			July 1, 1972 to June 30, 1974		
	Number of Requests	Percent of Total	Cumulative Percentage	Number of Requests	Percent of Total	Cumulative Percentage
1-50	12,001	27.5	27.5	5,155	11.7	11.7
51-100	5,499	12.6	40.1	3,058	6.9	18.6
101-150	3,741	8.6	48.7	2,327	5.3	23.9
151-200	2,868	6.6	55.3	2,111	4.8	28.7
201-250	2,299	5.3	60.6	1,879	4.3	33.0
251-300	1,999	4.6	65.2	1,658	3.8	36.8
301-350	1,668	3.8	69.0	1,512	3.4	40.2
351-400	1,435	3.3	72.3	1,314	3.0	43.2
401-450	1,257	2.9	75.2	1,221	2.8	45.0
451-500	1,115	2.6	77.8	1,133	2.6	48.6
501-550	976	2.2	80.0	1,022	2.3	50.9
551-600	882	2.0	82.0	934	2.1	53.0
601-650	781	1.8	83.8	855	1.9	54.9
651-700	689	1.6	85.4	796	1.8	56.7
701-750	579	1.3	86.7	780	1.8	58.5
751-800	507	1.2	87.9	742	1.7	60.2
801-850	442	1.0	88.9	683	1.5	61.7
851-900	370	0.8	89.7	644	1.5	63.2
Total for 900 most heavily used titles	39,108	89.7		27,824	63.2	
Total for all titles	43,582	100.0		44,203	100.0	

received, as contrasted with the almost 90 percent accounted for by the same number of periodicals in the first three years.

The other end of the distribution in both cases involves large numbers of periodicals very infrequently used. This is illustrated by a count of the number of periodicals for which there was only one request in five years. A total of 780 of these requests were made in the first three years and 2,348 in the last two years. This means that in the earlier period 750 heavily used periodicals accounted for 86.7 percent of the requests received, while 780 periodicals at the other extreme accounted for only 1.8 percent of the requests received. In the second period, 900 periodicals at one extreme accounted for 63.2 percent of the requests received, while more than two and a half times as many periodicals at the other extreme accounted for 5.3 percent of the requests received.

It seems reasonable to assume that the desire for access to periodical literature on the individual college campus is much like the patterns revealed by requests to the Periodical Bank, although the number of infrequently needed periodicals is presumably less. A periodical collection that would meet all needs would obviously be very large and would of necessity include many titles used very infrequently or not at all. Some combination of on-site access and access through interlibrary service is inevitable. The systematic collection and analysis of information on use seem to be the only effective ways of reaching rational decisions on the appropriate combination of these two access modes for the individual library. This means investment of time and money in the necessary research. The knowledge gained, however, should point the way to periodical acquisition and retention policies that would more than justify the investment required.

APPENDIX: ACM Periodical Bank

Heavily Used Periodicals and Number of Requests Received,
September 1, 1969, to June 30, 1974, in Order
of the Number of Requests Received

PERIODICAL	NUMBER OF REQUESTS
1) *Journal of Comparative and Physiological Psychology*	785
2) *Journal of Abnormal Psychology*	776
3) *Psychonomic Science*	690
4) *Journal of Experimental Psychology*	663
5) *American Journal of Psychiatry*	578
6) *America*	464
7) *Physiology and Behavior*	443
8) *American Journal of Psychology*	432
9) *Newsweek*	432
10) *Nature*	426
11) *American Journal of Physiology*	414
12) *Science*	402
13) *Biochemical and Biophysical Research Communications*	401
14) *New Republic*	380
15) *Science Digest*	380
16) *American Journal of Mental Deficiency*	351
17) *Psychological Reviews*	351
18) *Journal of Nervous and Mental Diseases*	329
19) *Economist*	329
20) *Science News*	316
21) *Archives of General Psychiatry*	315
22) *Time*	312
23) *Psychological Reports*	298
24) *Perceptual and Motor Skills*	294
25) *Perception and Psychophysics*	294
26) *New Statesman. London*	285
27) *Business Week*	282
28) *American Sociological Reviews*	280

PERIODICAL	NUMBER OF REQUESTS
29) *Nation*	279
30) *Journal of Genetic Psychology*	278
31) *Journal of Marriage and the Family*	268
32) *Journal of Psychology*	267
33) *Journal of Consulting and Clinical Psychology*	265
34) *Saturday Review*	264
35) *American Journal of Orthopsychiatry*	255
36) *Journal of Neurophysiology*	250
37) *School and Society*	242
38) *National Academy of Sciences. Proceedings*	241
39) *Contemporary Review*	240
40) *Biochemical Journal*	238
41) *American City*	237
42) *Journal of American Folklore*	234
43) *Senior Scholastic—Scholastic Teacher Edition*	233
44) *Journal of the American Medical Association*	219
45) *Journal of Physiology*	219
46) *Journal of Pharmacology and Experimental Therapeutics*	216
47) *Catholic World*	216
48) *Commonweal*	214
49) *Child Development*	211
50) *American Psychologist*	209
51) *Biochemistry (American Chemical Society)*	208
52) *Journal of Personality*	202
53) *Journal of Personality and Social Psychology*	201
54) *Endocrinology*	198
55) *American Journal of Sociology*	197
56) *World Today*	194
57) *U.S. News and World Report*	191
58) *Aviation Week and Space Technology*	191
59) *Economic History Review*	189

PERIODICAL	NUMBER OF REQUESTS
60) *Journal of General Physiology*	189
61) *Journal of Social Psychology*	188
62) *Modern Language Notes*	185
63) *Journal of Learning Disabilities*	183
64) *Journal of Experimental Child Psychology*	182
65) *Clearing House*	181
66) *Parent's Magazine*	179
67) *Psychosomatic Medicine*	178
68) *Psychological Bulletin*	177
69) *Biochimica et Biophysica Acta*	177
70) *New Outlook (New York)*	175
71) *Dissertation Abstracts*	174
72) *Gnomon*	174
73) *Journal of Cell Biology*	173
74) *Christian Century*	172
75) *Psychiatry*	172
76) *Human Relations, A Journal of Studies Towards the Interpretation of the Social Sciences*	172
77) *South Atlantic Quarterly*	171
78) *Journal of General Psychology*	170
79) *Hispania*	167
80) *Behaviour*	166
81) *Archives of Biochemistry and Biophysics*	165
82) *Education Digest*	163
83) *Spectator (London)*	162
84) *Reading Teacher*	159
85) *New York Academy of Sciences. Annals*	157
86) *Sociometry*	157
87) *Mental Hygiene*	153
88) *Scientific American*	153
89) *British Journal of Psychiatry*	151
90) *Journal of Clinical Psychology*	150
91) *Good Housekeeping*	148

PERIODICAL	NUMBER OF REQUESTS
92) *British Journal of Psychology*	147
93) *Journal of Chemical Physics*	146
94) *Social Problems*	146
95) *Studies in Philology*	145
96) *American Anthropologist*	145
97) *Acoustical Society of America. Journal*	144
98) *Social Forces*	141
99) *Atlantic Monthly*	140
100) *Journal of Organometallic Chemistry*	140
101) *Ebony*	139
102) *Developmental Psychology*	138
103) *New Yorker*	138
104) *Journal of Counseling Psychology*	137
105) *Russian Review*	132
106) *Trans-Action (Now Society)*	132
107) *American Mercury*	131
108) *Sociology and Social Research*	131
109) *Notes and Queries*	130
110) *Architectural Forum*	129
111) *Animal Behaviour*	128
112) *Journal of Mammology*	128
113) *Survey (New York)*	128
114) *Journal of Biological Chemistry*	126
115) *Behaviour Research and Therapy*	126
116) *Twentieth Century*	125
117) *Social Service Review*	124
118) *Archives of Neurology and Psychiatry*	124
119) *Elementary English*	122
120) *Nation's Business*	122
121) *Journal of Theoretical Biology*	121
122) *Commentary*	120
123) *Journal of Wildlife Management*	120
124) *Electroencephalography and Clinical Neurophysiology*	120

PERIODICAL	NUMBER OF REQUESTS
125) *National Review*	120
126) *Journal of Cellular Physiology*	119
127) *Reader's Digest*	119
128) *Ecological Monographs*	119
129) *E.L.H.*	117
130) *Music Journal*	117
131) *Journal of Applied Psychology*	116
132) *Hispanic Review*	115
133) *Journal of Verbal Learning and Verbal Behavior*	115
134) *Mind*	115
135) *Quarterly Journal of Studies on Alcohol*	114
136) *American Journal of Philology*	113
137) *Journal of English and Germanic Philology*	113
138) *Encounter. London*	113
139) *Philological Quarterly*	113
140) *Review of Reviews and World's Work*	112
141) *Research Quarterly*	111
142) *Sewanee Review*	110
143) *Biological Bulletin*	110
144) *Music Educators Journal*	110
145) *Social Research*	110
146) *University Review*	110
147) *Federation of American Societies for Experimental Biology. Federation Proceedings. Abstracts.*	110
148) *Today's Education*	109
149) *Experimental Cell Research*	109
150) *Psychology in the Schools*	107

Eugene Garfield

No-Growth Libraries and Citation Analysis; Or Pulling Weeds with Journal Citation Reports

Weeding is an old-fashioned term in library management, but there is still no process so painful to librarians. I have known several who could fire people more easily than they could discard books or journals.

Weeding a library is like examining an investment portfolio. Investment advisors know that people don't like to liquidate bad investments. How painful it is to realize that the hard-earned money you invested has not worked for you! Investment involves risk—and so does book and journal selection. Both types of risk-taking involve some speculation, a certain amount of guesswork, and a bit of hard information.

Just like frustrated tycoons, many librarians cannot face the fact that some of their guesses go wrong. They continue to throw good money after bad, hoping like so many optimistic stockbrokers that their bad decisions will somehow be undone. After paying for an unused journal for ten years, they rationalize that *maybe* someone will finally use it in the eleventh or twelfth year. It is difficult to buck the momentum inevitably gathered by a long-term subscription; it is so much easier to continue doing what has been done before.

In fact, the only object with enough inertial mass to stop this kind of irresistible force is an immovable budget. Weeding becomes essential during periods of stringency. Even in affluent times there is a limit to how much a library can buy. Nowadays the combined forces of information overload, inflation, and recession demand rigorous selection criteria.

This brings us to the concept of zero-growth for library collections, first presented in a stimulating paper by Daniel Gore in 1974.[1] Libraries simply cannot keep on growing exponentially. The tacit assumption that everything published must be acquired and kept is no longer tenable. The Alexandrian librarian who thinks there is a mandate to collect everything must soon face the reality that a truly complete collection is not—and never really *was*—possible.

To aspire to collect everything is characteristic of an archivist, whose job is to retain materials that are seldom, if ever, used. Of course, the function of a library is different from that of an archive. Most libraries, as distinct from archives, have little if any demand for aged material, and when they do, they usually know where and how it can be conveniently borrowed. Accessibility of material helps determine its frequency of use—and frequency of use *should* determine accessibility.

What has this to do with the nuts-and-bolts business of selecting books and weeding journals? Plenty.

The information explosion has come up against the inherent limitations of libraries—space, budget, and manpower. The resulting collision demands that libraries no longer be thought of as archival storehouses, but rather as bibliographic search centers. This implies two basic changes in priorities for library storage: first, from seldom-used documents to heavily used ones, and, second, from primary documents to all kinds of indexes and bibliographic tools.

Most libraries can afford to stress better bibliographic tools, even those that may be regarded as "too expensive" by traditional standards. For example, the cost of the *Science Citation Index* may displace subscriptions to only a few dozen marginally used journals. According to Williams and Pings[2], the *SCI* was in fact the "best investment" for hospital libraries.

Another change in libraries involves the process of weeding, or separating the seldom used material from the heavily used material. Let's first consider books.

As a book is cited each year, the probability increases that it will be used and cited again. If it has been cited fifty times, it has a high probability of being cited another fifty times. But, contrary to the intuitions of many librarians, if a book has never been cited it has a very low chance of ever being cited.

Keeping this in mind, ask yourself what kinds of books are likely to be donated to academic libraries. Are they the books that local scholars frequently consult? Or are they the books the donators never use, but nevertheless find difficult to throw away?

The bitter truth is that the supposed benefactors of libraries probably retain the books that they, and others, want to use again and again. Donated books often merely clutter shelves and increase the cataloging load. The library would actually be better off with a second copy of a frequently used book than with another book that no one will ever use.

Now let's consider journals.

According to the Bradford distribution, in almost any scientific field a small number of the journals publish a large percentage of cited articles.[3] Consider that 152 journals accounted for half of all reference citations to all scientific journals in the Institute for Science Information's (ISI) 1969 study.[4] More recent data show that the same relationship still holds (but with shifts in the ranks of the core journals). Therefore, the core of science and scholarship is relatively small in terms of numbers of journals. Numbers of articles is another matter. These same 152 core journals published only about 25 percent of all the articles, thus proving that we can and must be more selective.

Bradford's distribution tells us something about journal publication and interjournal citations. But my own law of concentration[5] shows that the same core journals dominate a large number of seemingly separate fields. Figure 1 is a matrix illustrating this point: the same group of journals turns up in a variety of medical and scientific specialties. The blank spaces indicate particular specialty journals of importance to only one field.

ISI's Journal Citation Reports (TM) shows that in the past decade the greatest growth in the literature was the result not so much of new journals as an increase in the number of articles in existing journals. Many new journals were simply expansions of existing ones: *The Journal of the Chemical Society of London* was divided into six separate sections, and the American Chemical Society journals spawned new titles like *Biochemistry*, which has quickly become a core journal.

What if citation frequency were made the sole criterion of selection? Massive weeding would have to follow. Out of the millions of journal articles that could be cited, one-third to one-half will never be cited. *Never.* These articles may be read, but not cited. In fact, according to Ackoff,[6] the average article is read by less than five people after it is published. Every librarian knows that some journal issues have never been touched by a single reader.

Assume for a moment that the world's literature of books and journals totals about 40 million titles. If you prefer, make it 50 million titles. My point is that only a fraction of 1 percent of all this material will ever be cited frequently enough to command the attention of library users. Thus, only 100,000 books and articles, or at the most 200,000, can form the active core of a library able to provide copies of 90 percent of all future citations.

This "rational" approach to journal collection can be taken a step further. Instead of using journals in their present form and arrangement, we might collect only reprints of highly cited articles. These would have the highest likelihood of being used again. Derek Price[7] has proposed a similar idea: publish a journal consisting entirely of heavily cited papers called the *Journal of Really Important Papers.*

The idea is not so farfetched. In fact, the cluster data that ISI is now compiling as part of its *ISI's Journal Citation Reports* will greatly facilitate the formation of such reprint collections. A group of libraries might get together to form a purchasing cooperative that could finance such reprinting on a large scale. I can imagine a collection of just 2,000 volumes, each containing twenty-five articles, that would satisfy 80 to 90 percent of a library's journal reference needs![8] Naturally, these initial 2,000 volumes would have to be augmented each year by about 5,000 newly identified items (about 200 volumes), both new and old, that had reached a specified citation threshold. But at the same time many of the articles in the original collection would fall below the citation threshold and would be discarded.

Such a core collection of heavily cited articles would comprise a true no-growth library. However, I suspect that most libraries would choose to store the heavily used articles even after they fell below the citation threshold. At least the library would now grow arithmetically rather than geometrically. Most libraries would probably compromise and would settle for linear growth—and would again periodically face the weeding problem.

FIGURE 1. Matrix showing citation relationship between the fifty most highly cited journals of science (excluding physics journals).

Listed in the legend column on the left are the fifty most highly cited journals of science, excluding physics journals, in order of the frequency of their citation by all journals. The vertical columns of the matrix show with a square slug whether each of the listed journals is itself among the fifty-journals most-highly cited by each.

1. JACS
2. J Biol Chem
3. Nature
4. J Chem Soc
5. Science
6. Bioc Biop A
7. P NAS USA
8. Biochem J
9. Lancet
10. CR Acad Sci
11. Am J Physiol
12. J Org Chem
13. Proc Soc
14. J Mol Biol
15. J Physiol L
16. P Roy Soc
17. J Cell Biol
18. J Clin Inv
19. J Phys Chem
20. Chem Ber
21. N Eng J Med
22. JAMA
23. Brit Med J
24. Analyt Chem
25. J Bact
26. Biochem
27. J Exp Med
28. Ann NY A Sci
29. Arch Bioc Biop
30. J Polym Sci
31. Bioc Biop R
32. Fed Proc
33. T Faraday
34. DAN SSSR
35. Circulation
36. Angew Chem
37. J Immunol
38. Inorg Chem
39. Circulation
40. Endocrinol
41. Acta Chem Sc
42. Nuov Cim
43. B S Ch Fr
44. Virology
45. Cancer R
46. Can J Chem
47. Helv Ch A
48. Z Naturf
49. Am J Med
50. J L Cl Med

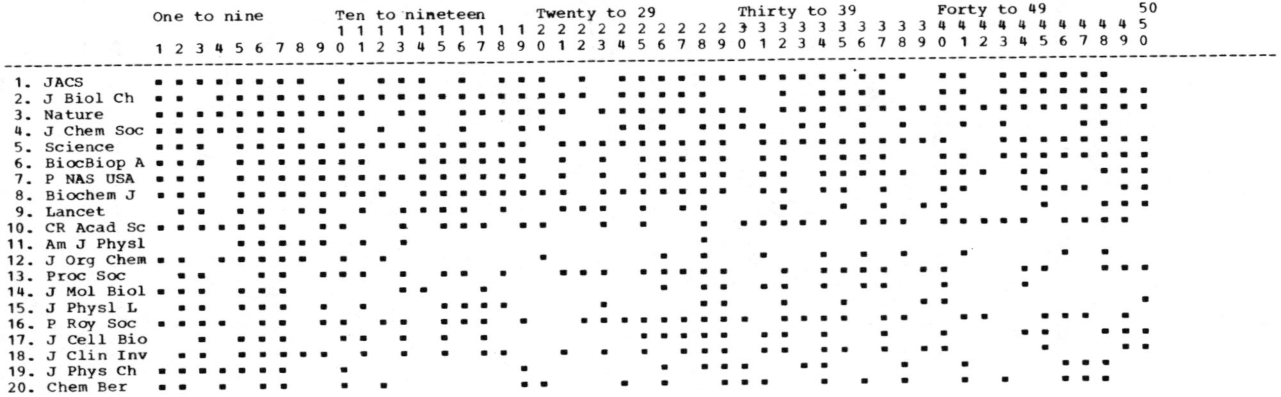

21. N Eng J M
22. JAMA
23. Br Med J
24. Analyt Ch
25. J Bact
26. Biochem
27. J Exp Med
28. Ann NY A S
29. Arc Bioc B
30. J Polym S
31. BiocBiop R
32. Fed P
33. T Faraday
34. DAN SSSR
35. J PET
36. Angew Ch
37. J Immunol
38. Inorg Che
39. Circulat
40. Endocrin
41. Act Chem S
42. Nuov Cim
43. B S Ch Fr
44. Virology
45. Cancer Res
46. Can J Chem
47. Helv Ch A
48. Z Naturf
49. Am J Med
50. J L Cl M

ISI has already begun the research necessary to identify, collect, publish, and market a core collection of heavily cited articles. Our cost estimates will be based on two important assumptions: that ISI would properly compensate publishers for use of their copyrighted materials, and that librarians providing hard-copy service of copyrighted materials would also compensate publishers.

In closing, I will read a letter published over three years ago by my colleague Melvin Weinstock:[9]

Sir,—In considering the application of Bradford's Law of Dispersion (1) as a guide to acquisition policy in the research library or information centre it is pleasant to contemplate a bibliophilic Utopia of a complete collection in a library with unlimited space and acquisition funds. Utopias are rarely found; however, and the library *does* have limited resources. Given this restriction, the librarian or acquisitions specialist, in even the largest and most pecunious libraries, must make choices. These choices are rational only to the extent that the library collection maximises the timely provision of requested documents to the satisfaction of the largest number of users.

In this light, A. Faser's letter (2) suggesting that a library is derelict in not purchasing a specialized journal of interest to only one user treats the occasional request with the same degree of importance as the on-going demand for the heavily used journals. An inventory policy in a department or food store, part-supply depot, manufacturing concern or library, based on ignoring frequency-of-demand distributions, leads to inefficient allocation of resources. Designers of sewer and flood control systems know they cannot design economic drainpipe and culvert systems of sufficient capacity to handle the runoff from the one-in-a-thousand chance that rainfall will exceed, say, 6 inches in any 1 hr period. And mass merchandisers stock only a few or no items in the extremely low and high size ranges of shoes, hats and all attire in between.

Bradford's Law promulgates that a library can supply *most* of the requests for material with a relatively modest inventory of book and journal titles, geared to the *normal* pattern of demand. This demand pattern is one in which a relatively few items from among all possible items in the inventory satisfy a majority of the actual transactions. Progressively fewer transactions are satisfied from the balance of the inventory, or from further augmentation of the number of titles held. Abiding by the Bradford distribution, then, is an important factor in the library's overall success at demand-fulfillment.

The most efficient way for a library to exploit its collection and maximize utilization of its document file is to share its bibliographic resources with as many patrons as possible. It cannot *reasonably* be expected to serve *every* individual request. Carried to the extreme, if the only requests were one-time requests, there could not be an *economic* central library. The most efficient way of handling such a situation would be for each individual to have his own private collection.

Yours faithfully,

MELVIN WEINSTOCK

Institute for Scientific Information
325 Chestnut Street
Philadelphia,
Pennsylvania 19106
1.Fairthorne, A., *J. Doc.*, 25,319 (1969).
2.Faser A., *Nature* 227,101 (1970).

Many scientists assume that librarians make no judgments whatsoever in journal selection, that they are a captive market. While it is true that many librarians have been guilty of poor administration of their journal collection, it is also true that they have had only a minimum of hard data to work with. Fortunately, it is now possible to distinguish among books and journals with accuracy, precision, and objectively. Thus, it is possible to make more scientific decisions.

Notes

1. D. Gore, "Zero Growth for the College Library," *College Management* 9, (August-September 1974): 12-14.
2. J.F. Williams and V.M. Pings, "A Study of the Access to the Scholarly Record from a Hospital Health Science Core Collection," Report No. 54, Wayne State University, School of Medicine, Library and Biomedical Information Service Center, Detroit, Michigan, January 1970.
3. S. C. Bradford, *Documentation* (Washington, D.C.: Public Affairs Press, 1950), 156 pp.

4. E. Garfield, "Citation Analysis As a Tool in Journal Evaluation," *Science* 178 (1972): 471-479.

5. E. Garfield, "The Mystery of the Transposed Journal Lists—Wherein Bradford's Law of Scattering Is Generalized According to Garfield's Law of Concentration," *Current Contents*, No. 31 (1971): 5-6.

6. M. H. Halbert and R. L. Ackoff, "An Operations Research Study of the Dissemination of Scientific Information," in *Proceedings of the International Conference on Scientific Information, Washington, D.C. November 16-21, 1958* (Washington, D.C.: National Academy of Sciences, 1958), vol. 1, pp. 97-130.

7. D. Price, "Networks of Scientific Papers," *Science* 149 (1965): 510-515.

8. M. B. Line, A. Sandison, and J. MacGregor, *Patterns of Citations to Articles Within Journals; A Preliminary Test of Scatter, Concentration and Obsolescence*, Bath University Reports (Bath: Bath University Library Report No. 2, October 1972), 33 pp., ISBN 0 900843 27 6.

9. M. Weinstock, "Bradford's Law," Letter to the Editor of *Nature* 233 (1971): 434.

William L. Corya *and* *Michael K. Buckland*

Automation and Collection Control

Although the main theme of this conference is strategies for stemming library growth, this paper will attempt to show how automation impacts library growth both positively and negatively. The effect of automation on libraries as they increase in size will also be discussed.

Our basic premise is that automation of library processes and access to computer-based files tend mainly to encourage library growth, but the byproducts of such processing and computer-based access tend to stem or control growth if used systematically. Is it not true that the main reason for applying computers to library problems is to cope with growth, not curb it? Most automation projects are developed on the grounds that future growth can be handled with little or no increase in expenditure and that new and improved service can be offered as more materials become available. This seems only to encourage library growth because of the promise that, no matter how large files and materials inventories grow, computers will be able to cope with the size of the materials collection and the files associated with it. Computers, when applied to library processing jobs, simply make it too easy to grow—and appear to contribute almost nothing toward controlling library growth. Therefore, in light of this unexpected dilemma, the remainder of this paper will examine two basic areas of automation as applied to libraries: the technical processing (or computer-based access) applications and the "control" applications. As used here, technical processing means the application of computers to perform actual library processes wherever found in the library, and control means the application of computer-based and computer-generated data to provide decision-making information for management purposes.

Technical Processing

By now most people in the library field are aware of the areas where automation has been applied in libraries to handle traditional processing functions. These are generally based on a one-to-one handling of a previously manual task. Since many of these projects have been reported in the literature, there is no real need to list them here. Suffice it to say that attempts have been made to automate most library processing tasks.

As soon as a process is automated, a large amount of data begins accumulating and a data base begins to be built. At this point, even though the processing task itself has been accomplished, access to the accumulated raw data resulting from the task becomes available. For instance, an automated circulation system may be implemented mainly to handle the actual circulation transactions of charging, discharging, and overdues preparation. However, the fact that data on each title in the library system are now in machine-readable form and can be accessed by a computer system opens up the possibility of providing many additional products. Although programming is necessary for every task performed by a computer system, a variety of special listings of the data base becomes feasible.

As an example, the accumulated data base can be offered to any number of locations either within or outside the specific library system. In a batch system, computer-printed listings could be distributed; in an on-line system, the availability of a computer terminal would have a similar effect. In other words, the duplication of files and data becomes a relatively easy task for an automated system.

The Ohio College Library Center (OCLC) can be used as an example of how an automated process can have both negative and positive effects on library growth. It has been demonstrated that OCLC can displace expensive manual cataloging and card-production tasks. At the same time, it has encouraged library growth (or at least it has not discouraged it) by making it easy and cost-effective to add as many new titles as desired. But by duplicating the contents of the data base through all the remote terminals in the system, it has also facilitated the curbing of library growth by advertising the fact that an item being considered for acquisition by one library might already be available at another location close enough to be borrowed. This same situation would exist on a smaller basis in a multilibrary system in a college or university where the mere fact that an item is known to be available nearby might be enough to discourage the buying of additional copies.

Another byproduct of automating a process is the ability to manipulate or rearrange the accumulated data base in any desired format.[1] The data can be arranged in almost any manner imagined, and all or any part of the data can be included. When users really understand this capability, requests for manipulated data in every conceivable format are likely to pour into the Systems Office. An example of such a system at Purdue is the Serials Catalog System,[2] where the data base can be presented in many useful ways to library staff and users, even though the basic goal of the system design was to produce just one main sequence of the data. To illustrate, the data may be arranged by title, call number, or location, with each entry showing any or all of the associated data such as single or multiple sets held, receipt status, bibliographic notes, cross-references, and special location within a library. Using OCLC again as an example, it is doubtful that it would be enjoying such popularity if it were only able to accept cataloging input and simply create one large catalog file of all titles that could *not* be manipulated to reproduce the distinctive catalog-card layouts of individual member libraries.

Compare this ability to manipulate data with the unit card or printed catalog where rearranging data into a different format or presenting it in a different sequence is difficult, expensive, and time-consuming. The Purdue Serials Catalog System just mentioned is an example of a system that has not significantly reduced processing time or cost. The *byproducts* of the process, however, have been a valuable improvement to services and probable control of serials growth through the provision of the data base at multiple locations and in various formats for help in making purchase and cancellation decisions.

Another byproduct of the computer's ability to manipulate data is that of creating special subsets of the data. For example, with the Purdue Serials Catalog System it is possible to produce a selection of subsets such as a holdings list of any one of the departmental libraries, or a list of titles received as gift subscriptions, exchanges, etc.

Creation of a large data base such as that at OCLC could in itself be valuable as an interlibrary loan service. The real value of such an automated system, however, is its ability to create subsets of data either in catalog card format or as magnetic tape records for further manipulation, or printed catalogs or other forms associated with individual libraries or specific classes of data. Admittedly, this is not a revelation about OCLC or any other automated system, but it does point out that the ability of automated systems to cope with special needs tends to encourage library growth by making such growth affordable from a processing standpoint.

Automating a particular process certainly has other implications for library growth, besides the ability to create a variety of byproduct listings and files. File searching is a major area affected by computer-based access. In fact, a desire to increase search efficiency (for file maintenance and information retrieval) seems to have been one of the major reasons for computerization. It is well known that the cost of searching manual files increases steadily as the size of the file increases. It is simply a matter of having to examine more records to get to the desired one. But in a computer-based system, especially in cooperative systems such as OCLC, the unit costs of searching for a particular record in the file rise much more slowly, if at all, as the size of the file increases. Depending on the pricing structure and the distribution of costs in a *cooperative* situation, the cost might even decrease as the size of the file increases and more locations are added. Again, this leveling off or decrease of unit costs provided by a computer-based system as file size increases does not discourage library growth. New money, that in a manual system would be spent on increased personnel costs, is now available for purchase of new materials.

Circulation files are good examples of the comparison of unit costs in manual and computer systems. Although reshelving and check in/out unit costs would likely not be affected by automation unless some self-service items such as lightpens were introduced, the maintenance and searching of circulation files themselves are definitely affected by automation. The maintenance and searching of manual files become almost unmanageable and costly as they grow, whereas a computer-based file is not so affected.

Pre-order searching and verification and cataloging are other good examples of increased unit costs as file sizes increase in the manual system. On the other hand, computer-based access of such files helps to keep costs level, if not to decrease them, as the size of the file grows. This is another case of coping with growth and the additional technical processing it demands, and thereby not discouraging constant increase in collection size.

Modification and updating of files and records are another major area where automation can make a significant impact on library growth. With manual systems, it is so costly and time-consuming to change or remove records of discarded materials, many libraries avoid weeding altogether, especially those libraries that have grown rapidly. It may be cheaper to store unused materials indefinitely than to discard them or move them to another location.[3] With a computer-based system, this task becomes relatively easy and cost-effective since, once the change in the master record has been made, all listings, indexes, catalogs, and the like can be changed automatically. The ease with which an automated system can be utilized to discard and retire materials to other less expensive locations can help control library growth by permitting the librarian to be less hesitant about changing the location of materials.

Moving materials in and out of different collections and storage facilities, as suggested by Salton[4] in his "dynamic library," is facilitated by the ease with which records can be modified or even discarded in an automated system. This kind of status-changing is probably not even possible with manual record-keeping systems, even if appropriate management data were available on which to base such decisions.

The increasing availability of large bibliographical data bases also touches on the question of library growth. Although the availability of these data bases at remote sites by terminals is essentially the same situation as the "duplication of files" mentioned earlier, the effect may not always be to buy fewer journals, books, and other materials. It may be just the opposite. The speed with which a remote data base can be searched may not be much of an improvement over manual searching in the user's eyes if the library still has to wait several days to obtain the document. In other words, more pressure may be brought to purchase more of the exotic materials that turn up all the time in such searches. If the data base can be searched quickly, why can't the documents be delivered quickly?

But, as mentioned earlier, the probable effect of remote data bases such as OCLC, MEDLINE, and Lockheed will be one of satisfaction that an item is definitely known to exist somewhere where it can be borrowed in a relatively short time. If searching of a remote data base can be coupled with location data (which the CONSER project[5] is presumably moving toward), then the availability of such data through improved interlibrary loan services will probably discourage library growth and competition to the extent that cooperation actually develops.

So much for the technical process applications of automation and the many byproducts they can generate. Thus far, all of the products and advantages of automation mentioned are made possible merely by the fact that computer-accessed data can be duplicated, manipulated, and broken into any number of subsets, employing the same data used in the automation of the process at hand. The only decision required is whether to program in order to produce a listing on paper, microform, CRT screen, or whatever. The effect on library growth has been shown to be varied and somewhat unpredictable. In some cases, such as interlibrary loan and discarding, automation can be said to facilitate a curbing of growth, but for the most part it seems to make growth easier to cope with and thus does not discourage it.

Control

Automating a procedure or function might be valuable in itself if it would eliminate one or more persons from the task, or possibly avoid future personnel increases and costs. Would it be even more valuable, however, if it could also eliminate, for example, an entire departmental or branch library, or if it could provide the information needed for systematic discarding? This is where the control aspect of computer-based systems begins to pay the way for automation. The data needed for control purposes may also be the very same data used in the technical process, or it may be, as is often the case, data generated as a sidelight of the process concerning processing times, costs, demand, usage, and the like. *The control function of an automated system may turn out to be much more valuable as far as providing better service and keeping costs and growth to a minimum than the automation of the process itself.* Certainly the potential control information generated by a computer-based access system is the largest factor in automation that might control library growth.

Numerous articles have been written about computer-generated management information and its usefulness as control data for an organization. When this kind of data was first discovered as a valuable byproduct of computer-based access, it was believed that the computer itself would be able to take over some of the routine de-cision-making or process control. Large management information systems were envisioned. Although this is still an ultimate goal for utilizing management information, many of the early dreams have since been tempered by reality: decision-makers are not quite sure what data are needed and what those data mean. It should be stressed, however, that this type of thinking, while quite common in industry, has been largely absent from the literature of librarian-ship.

In libraries, computer-generated management information can be a valuable management tool if appropriate data can be first of all identified, then interpreted, and finally used effectively. A basic prob-lem with today's libraries is that most services are performed much the same way as they always have been (although the computer now helps the process along somewhat), with little response to the changing needs, habits, and values of users and potential users. This is where the mass of data generated by the computer-based system can really be put to work to minimize costs, control growth, and dras-tically improve the services offered to users. The dynamic library sit-uation described by Salton[6] clearly portrays how responsive a li-brary could and should be if management data were applied in a meaningful way. One of Salton's basic principles of a dynamic li-brary situation is that it be "an adaptive environment in which the user population influences the main intellectual processes such as the indexing vocabulary and practices, the storage organization, the search and retrieval operations, and, finally, the collection control necessitated by document growth and retirement."

Almost without fail, most published descriptions of library auto-mation projects and general discussions of library automation *men-tion* the fact that management information is a real advantage of library automation. Unfortunately, determining precisely what data should be collected, how it should be analyzed and presented, and the significance of it are generally left vague. Operations research stud-ies are becoming more common, but as yet seem to have contributed relatively little toward developing practical models upon which de-cisions can be reliably based. If nothing else, this paper should issue a challenge to library administrators to commit their energies to iden-tifying relevant management data and determining through research effort its significance for better library service, both in terms of min-imizing costs and providing effective service to users. The primary goal of all administrators should be to provide library service that will be responsive to changing user demands and needs. Management data generated as a byproduct of computer based systems is a prime source for such responsiveness.

One significant area where control data can be generated and applied is in acquisitions and materials processing. Data generated from an automated order system can be used to monitor purchasing patterns, vendor responsiveness, publisher trends, average costs, unit costs, subject selection habits of various classes of selectors, departmental buying habits, budget allocations, total processing, peak loads, delays, and all kinds of comparisons of the various categories of data. [7] The possibilities of generating almost any kind of data imaginable are real in an automated environment, but applying these data to decision-making is the real challenge.

Data derived from an automated technical processing system are indeed useful both for improving the processes themselves and for providing better user services and responsiveness to the users. However, there seems to be little doubt that the circulation processes of the library generate the really meaningful data needed for providing dynamic, user-responsive library services. The possibilities for use of circulation data from an automated system are far-reaching. These data are, we believe, the basic information needed to control library growth and maintain collections for the most effective uses.

Data concerning user characteristics, subject matter and age of materials requested and borrowed, subsequent use of the materials, peak and average circulation loads, location of request correlated with location of materials (in an on-line system), length of use of materials, reservations of materials during specific time periods, unfulfilled requests, types of interlibrary loans, and any other aspect of user behavior or collection characteristic can potentially be used to control and maintain an effective collection. Several studies have examined the data derivable from automated circulation systems and have applied these data to developing policies and decision points concerning circulation loan periods, availability, duplication, and retirement of materials. [8] An example of practical application of data derived from computer-based circulation is at the University of Lancaster where variable loan periods were developed that react to the use patterns of each and every item in the library stock. [9] Another example is at the University of Pennsylvania where a separate special collection—the separateness of which had been considered essential for several years—was merged into the general collection as a direct result of data generated by an automated circulation system. [10] This does not mean that the computer made the decision, but it does indicate that only the automated system can handle the mass of data needed to provide reliable information as a basis for a well-informed decision.

Management data derived from automated circulation systems is a powerful factor in maintaining collections and controlling growth through the establishment of a hierarchy of library collections. Depending on the use patterns of individual library materials, a structure can be developed which reliably places materials in various levels of maintenance and availability, such as a reserve collection, a working collection, a stored collection, and the materials outside the library system that must be borrowed through interlibrary loan. Circulation data can be constantly monitored to create a dynamic situation where the size of the libraries and the materials held can be designed and adjusted to different levels depending on the levels of, and changes in, use and demand patterns. [11]

Salton [12] proposes that use data can be applied even further. He believes that a dynamic library should react to changes in use patterns with not just changes in borrowing availability but in classification and indexing. This kind of responsiveness in a large collection appears, of course, to be possible only through the use of computer-based access systems.

This, then, is a glimpse of the control aspect of computer-based systems. It appears that this use of automated systems has slipped in the back door as processes have been automated with the objectives of speeding up handling, coping with the increased load of library growth, and curbing rising personnel costs. As stated earlier, this kind of reliable management data, never before available, may contribute significantly to controlling library growth. It may turn out to be automation's greatest contribution to solving library problems.

Notes

1. Allen B. Veaner, "Institutional Political and Fiscal Factors in the Development of Library Automation, 1967-71," *Journal of Library Automation* 7, no. 1 (March 1974): 5-26.
2. William L. Corya, and Gary C. Lelvis, "The Purdue University Serials Catalog System," *Computerized Serials Systems Series* (LARC) 1, no. 4 (1974).

3. Ralph E. Ellsworth, *The Economics of Book Storage in College and University Libraries* (Metuchen, N.J.: Association of Research Libraries and Scarecrow Press, 1969).

4. Gerald Salton, "Proposals for a Dynamic Library," *Information: Part 2—Reports, Bibliographies* 2, no. 3 (1973): 1-27.

5. Richard Anable, "CONSER: An Update," *Journal of Library Automation* 8, no. 1 (March 1975): 26-30.

6. Salton, "Proposals for a Dynamic Library."

7. R. M. Duchesne, "Analysis of Costs and Performance," *Library Trends* 21, no. 4 (April 1973): 587-603. R. M. Duchesne, "Library Management Information from Computer-aided Library Systems," in A. G. Mackenzie and I. M. Stuart, eds., *Planning Library Services: Proceedings of a Research Seminar, Lancaster, 1969*, University of Lancaster Library Occasional Papers, 3 (Lancaster, England: University Library, 1969). (ERIC report ED-045-173.) John Lubans, Jr., *A Study with Computer Based Circulation Data of the Non-use and Use of a Large Academic Library. Final Report.* June 1973. Colorado University Libraries, Boulder, Colorado. (ERIC Report ED-082-756.) Robert W. Burns, Jr., "An Empirical Rationale for the Accumulation of Statistical Information," *Library Resources and Technical Services* 18, no. 3 (Summer 1974): 253-258.

8. Peter Simmons, *Collection Development and the Computer: A Case Study in the Analyses of Machine Readable Loan Records and Their Application to Book Selection* (Vancouver, University of British Columbia, 1971). M. K. Buckland, *Book Availability and the Library User* (New York: Pergamon, 1975). P. M. Morse, *Library Effectiveness: A Systems Approach* (Cambridge, Mass.: MIT Press, 1968).

9. Buckland, *Book Availability and the Library User.*

10. Personal communication with Bob Kearney, Library Systems Analyst, University of Pennsylvania Libraries, in 1973.

11. I. Woodburn, "A Mathematical Model of a Hierarchical Library System," in A. G. Mackenzie and I.M. Stuart, eds., *Planning Library Services: Proceedings of a Research Seminar, Lancaster, 1969*, University of Lancaster Library Occasional Papers, 3 (Lancaster, England: University Library, 1969). (ERIC report ED-045-173.) B. C. Brookes, "The Design of Cost-effective Hierarchical Information Systems," *Information Storage and Retrieval* 6, no. 2 (June 1970): 127-136. B. C. Brookes, "The Viability of Branch Libraries," *Journal of Librarianship* 2, no. 1 (January 1970): 14-21. R. E. Coughlin, F. Taïeb, and B. H. Stevens, *Urban Analysis for Branch Library System Planning* (Westport Conn.: Greenwood Press, 1972). W. B. Pitt, D. H. Kraft, and L. B. Heilprin, "Buy or Copy? A Library Operations Research Model." *Information Storage and Retrieval* 10, no. 9/10 (September-October 1974): 331-341.

12. Salton, "Proposals for a Dynamic Library."

MODERATED BY **Dan Martin**

PRESIDENT OF THE ASSOCIATED COLLEGES
OF THE MIDWEST

PANELISTS: *CRAIG BAZZANI, RAY HEFFNER,*

JOSEPH SEMROW, AND *ALPHONSE TREZZA*

Opportunities and obstacles along the road to the no-growth, high-performance library

A PANEL DISCUSSION

MODERATOR: I am deliberately billed on your program as moderator rather than chairman because you have before you an uncommonly obstreperous panel, and I will do my best to moderate what I hope will be their altogether intemperate views.

The gladiators here before you are to my right Craig Bazzani, who is chief of the Higher Education Unit in the Illinois Bureau of the Budget in Springfield, and at his right Joseph Semrow, executive director of the North Central Association of Colleges and Schools. To my left is Al Trezza who is now executive director of the National Commission on Libraries and Information Science, but is known to most of us as the state librarian of Illinois; and at his left is Ray Heffner, who is currently professor of English at the University of Iowa. Ray is here as a humanistic scholar, but his previous experience as academic vice-president at Iowa and similarly at Indiana, and as president of Brown University gives him an administrative point of view as well.

After opening remarks from the panelists, each will have an opportunity to rebut one another and then we'll turn to rebuttal, cries of outrage, and other indications of horror from the floor.

So let me begin first at the extreme right (this is not a political spectrum here) and ask Joe Semrow to lead off.

MR. JOSEPH SEMROW: I am just one person representing the field of accrediting, and it is a bit difficult because the North Central Association is just one of six regional accrediting associations in the country. In addition to that, there are about thirty-five to forty-five professional or specialized accrediting agencies, each with its own particular standards. In addition to that group of thirty-five or forty-five, recognized by the old National Commission on Accrediting which has now gone out of existence, there are about sixty agencies recognized by the United States Office of Education which are authorized to carry on accreditation or recognition activities.

So I am speaking, I guess, mainly from what I know of the North Central Association and the other five regional accrediting agencies.

All of the agencies vary somewhat in their approach. In the beginning of the accrediting movement, around the turn of the century, most of the agencies employed what we call standards for accreditation; this was largely to distinguish institutions of higher or post-secondary education, the term we use now, from secondary schools. Over the years, there has been a movement away from what we call the standardizing or normative approach in accrediting, where one says "You must do this, and have that, to be accredited." What we have evolved today is a kind of problem-solving approach through institutional self-study, and this represents a correlation of institutional objectives with institutional outcomes.

Listening to the speakers at this conference, I think there is probably a very strong carryover among librarians of the normative approach to accrediting. Thus, one might say, for example, that a community college of a certain size and type must have 20,000 books; or 5 percent of the budget of an institution must be devoted to the library. Or a certain collection size will be required for doctoral-degree granting institutions. Incidentally, in the North Central area itself, over the past ten or fifteen years, we have had about 100 institutions move from the baccalaureate- or master-degree granting stages to the doctoral-degree granting stages.

I was just thinking that if our approach had remained a standard-setting approach, in which we actually did encourage all institutions to aspire to become members through standards espoused, for example, by the Association of Research Libraries or some similar organization, I don't know if mass confusion would be the result, or chaos or bankruptcy or what. I think one of the greatest things we can do as an accrediting agency is to help the institutions that we work with to understand that accreditation is concerned with the development of institutional objectives and self-assessment of performance, and to dispel as much as we can the notion that we are accrediting according to certain rule-of-thumb measures or for certain standards such as percentages, and this kind of thing. Hopefully, in joining with the other regional accrediting associations, and also with the other specialized and professional accrediting agencies, we can develop some more helpful and meaningful approaches to evaluation and accreditation.

MODERATOR: Thank you very much, Joe. We turn next to Ray Heffner.

MR. RAY HEFFNER: I don't know whether I am here mainly as a professor of English, and, therefore, as one of the most obstreperous and highly critical of the users of the library, or as an ex-provost and university president, in which jobs I not only had budget discussions with the director of University Libraries, but also, of course, was the chief receiver of gripes from all segments of the campus; or perhaps as the former chairman of the Committee on Institutional Cooperation of the Big Ten Universities in Chicago, in which job I was a vigorous promoter of cooperative solutions to all problems, particularly library problems; or perhaps as North Central examiner and consultant.

You just heard Joe Semrow on accreditation, but I have a word or two to add about that.

I know now why I have been assigned to inspect libraries for the North Central on several accreditation visits, because in one this week I was successful in finding the skeleton in the librarian's closet. This was quite literally so, and since we had been talking about pilferage, the librarian pointed out to me that the poor skeleton had lost its skull some years back. But the main point of interest to me was that that skeleton had arrived as a teaching exhibit for some anthropology professor who no longer used it, and where does it end up? In the librarian's closet to be maintained in perpetuity. Now that it has lost its skull, of course, it has lost its interest and has been sent to the library.

I think it is possible that associations for accreditation have been responsible for some of the problems you have been addressing yourselves to. Despite the fact that I fully share Joe Semrow's statement that we don't want to cause such problems, and we try to deal with in-

stitutional goals as individual entities and to relate to them, nevertheless, there are some very effective myths about accreditation, and they
function more than the facts. For example, almost any member of the
law faculty on your campus will say to the authorities that they will
lose their law school accreditation if the law library is not a free-
standing unit. If it is integrated into the general library system, they
cannot be accredited. Nonsense! The AALS has told me that is not so.
You can't find it in any manual, but it is a fact that this myth helps to
create an inefficiency which you want to get rid of but can't.

Also, of course, the fact that there are concrete standards is still an
operative myth. In one accreditation visit in which I was engaged
recently, they were talking about how the budget is allocated and how
it is spent, and one of the bibliographers, a liaison librarian, was talking to me, and he said, "Oh, yes, I am seeing that this much money
gets spent."

He said, "It's a hard job for me to persuade those faculty members
that they need that many books, but I assure you that I am living up to
the standard, and I am getting that money spent on acquisitions every
year just as you want me to."

Well, we need a great deal of general education and publicity to
overcome that misconception.

Perhaps Dan even found out that there is a skeleton in my closet, for
way back when I was a junior at Yale, I served as a librarian for one of
the Yale residential colleges. I think it was the most pleasant job I
have ever had. Ever since then I have felt that when I left university
administration to be a full-time professor, I was going to retreat into
the library and away from management information systems. So I
have been a little appalled to find that they are creeping into the library, that wonderful retreat where I thought books were loved for
their own sake rather than data for its sake.

I have a few confessions to make. I have borrowed books from the
library that I have not read, and I have read books that I have not
borrowed. I have used books that I have neither borrowed nor read.
As a matter of fact, I think sometimes the very physical presence on
the shelf of books that you don't use is a very effective mechanism for
selecting the book that you do read. I like to browse, although I realize
that in a university library where faculty have almost unlimited withdrawal privileges and all graduate students have semester privileges,
the chance of finding what is central to my field in browsing on the
shelf is very minimal indeed. Nevertheless, I go and browse. There-

fore, I get into some of the more exotic material that nobody else wants to read, I suppose.

Well, I will go back then and wear primarily the hat of the professor of English and the unashamed Alexandrian.

I was delighted to find in Dan Gore's article the name for what I have been. I can now say proudly that I am an Alexandrian. I don't think I ever threw a book in my private library away in my life. I don't think I ever will. And the only perfect library to me is the complete library, the one that has everything.

I have been a little upset here to hear so many times that the function of the library is to support the faculty and the academic program of the institution. Well, I hope that in many cases libraries are subverting the faculty and the academic program because it could very well be possible that the faculty at any moment in time is terribly limited in its vision. They don't really understand very deeply the subject that they are professing to teach, and only a well-run, well-organized library collection will correct all the misinformation that they are feeding the students in the classroom.

So if you tie a library too closely to your academic program, you may be putting the students into tunnels, giving them all kinds of cattle chutes which will lead them to slaughter but not to the kind of comprehensive education you hoped for.

Now I acknowledge that my experience has been at major universities, but I think it's a myth that the kind of library I am talking about is only relevant for research purposes and for research institutions. I don't think so. I think the kind of library I am talking about, which has an integrity of its own, which has a teaching function to perform, is much more significant for undergraduate students. The research specialist can use what information retrieval or interlibrary loan or other complex bibliographic assistance you want to provide, and he can structure his life so that he can wait the time for that book to come from some place else. It is the undergraduate student who really doesn't know quite how the subject is organized who can most benefit from a well-established collection and from a well-run library. Hence, recognizing that my Alexandrian ideal is going to be very difficult to achieve, and that we will have to have some weeding, what kind of priorities would I place on how that weeding is taking place?

Probably the best way would be some random selection of the books that you have to get rid of. The worst way would be to ask your faculty to weed it for you, because that will produce the kind of tunnel vision that I am talking about.

Well, what I guess I am finally arguing for is that, even in liberal arts colleges with relatively small libraries, we may have to have several collections: one to support the curriculum; another, a very limited research collection for rapid access to some research materials that might be used either by advanced students or by faculty members; but then, third, a teaching collection that is organized out of a sense of integrity and mission by library professionals who see that they are themselves teachers and have something to contribute to that college that is not just backing up others or providing access to somebody else's library. [Applause]

MODERATOR: Thank you, Ray. I think it may well be altogether fitting that after that buoyant vision, we turn to the heavy in our act here in the person of Craig Bazzani, who asks questions about where the dollars come from and where they go—particularly the public revenue dollars.

MR. CRAIG BAZZANI: I am not really sure whose perspective I am supposed to take or will end up taking, but I guess I can speak for the taxpayers and all levels of government and students. I think that pretty much covers everybody who pays money into the universities, at least some of which goes into libraries.

While nobody elected me to public office, and I can't speak for a governor or a legislator, I can say from the taxpayer's perspective, at least, and certainly in the 1970s, that we have got to take a harder look at higher education generally, and specifically at some of the elements within university operations, on a day-to-day basis.

To understand what generally is happening to higher education, one needs to look at the competition for what is becoming very scarce dollars at all governmental levels.

Higher education is today having to compete with elementary and secondary education, which are predominantly supported by local property taxes that people are unwilling to raise. There is more and more reliance on state government. You are competing with mental health and public health. Public aid and welfare costs are probably skyrocketing more than anything else. So higher education still has a place in the sun, but there are some clouds floating by, and I think it may be some time before things return to normalcy.

The national trends that we see surfacing today indicate that higher education continues to get more new dollars year in and year out, but, as a percentage of total state budgets, that support has been declining.

That is certainly true in Illinois, even though we have set a record budget for higher education. Higher education in Illinois has a lower priority than it once had.

Within higher education itself, there are other adverse economic factors.

The first is enrollment decline. Birth rates have tapered off and enrollment rates within a typical college population have declined, so we are seeing enrollments decline.

That obviously has to have some impact on long-range planning over the next fifteen or twenty years.

The next constraint is the new mix of institutions we see emerging. Community colleges and vocational groups are eating up more and more of the student numbers. Community colleges are close to home. Costs are somewhat lower. Vocational schools have good job placement records with graduates.

It is a capsule-type education, and the senior universities where we spend a lot of money on research and library development are having a hard time justifying new increments in their budgets when they are competing even within their own sector for the new dollars.

Employability of graduates is a third constraint. I checked Bureau of Labor Statistics reports recently and found that about 15 percent of humanities, social sciences, and education graduates can't find jobs. Of the 85 percent who do, less than half are employed in anything that is closely related to what they were trained to do, and that kind of information plays on the minds of governors and educators and university administrators.

Fourth, changing manpower needs. We see a new emergence of health education, social-justice type programs, recreation, park administration, bilingual education, computer science, and, to a lesser extent, accounting and engineering are back on the way, and obviously, that has some relevance to long-range planning for libraries.

Other constraints include inflation, especially in a labor-intensive industry such as teaching and librarianship.

The last constraint is what I call the ivory tower syndrome. It may be a constraint that is more important today than ever before with governors and legislators. These people look at university faculty working twelve hours a week, and wonder why they cannot be more productive.

One college president this year, negotiating a budget level, said, "I absolutely cannot do one thing more without additional funds," and from the state level we just don't think that is a very salable argument. There is some anti-intellectual sentiment in state houses around the country, and you ought to be aware of it, because it will filter down through your libraries.

From what I have seen up to this point, I have been impressed, nonetheless, with the open-mindedness of those of you in attendance at the conference, especially librarians. I think you have demonstrated that you have the tools to meet some of these challenges, to identify with critical masses, to cause some reallocations and productivity increases to take place, and to enter into cooperative agreements with sister institutions or maybe neighboring institutions to try to reduce some of these costs that you just simply can't avoid. These are the very same sorts of things that state government and national government are asking higher education to do, and I commend the efforts you have made at this conference.

MODERATOR: Thank you, Craig. Let's turn quickly now to Al Trezza whom I have been saving until last.

MR. ALPHONSE TREZZA: Of course, today I am speaking in my capacity as executive director of the National Commission on Libraries and Information Science, and not from my post from which I am on leave, which is director of the Illinois State Library. But a lot of my comments, obviously, will apply to both because in Illinois we have a total state cooperative program. Consequently, a lot of the things the Commission is trying to do have been mirrored in Illinois and other states as well.

The National Commission is faced with the total problem of providing the information that the nation as a whole needs. How do you make sure that any citizen, be he farmer, minority person, scholar, loafer, you name them, has the same opportunity of access to material and of getting it reasonably quickly, just as you do in your university or college libraries, or in your public libraries, as the case may be? In other words, information in the libraries is not for the intellectually or economically or culturally elite, but for everyone.

One of the big criticisms we get is exactly that, that we are now working too hard to feed the haves, not the have-nots. That is an easy criticism to make, but difficult to prove and to offset. Nevertheless, you have to keep that in the back of your mind as one of the problems.

So the Commission in looking at the national program says: How do we share resources? How do we do a better job of making them available?

We frankly say we need a national program, and as most of you in the audience know, the Commission is in the process of producing a national program. It is called "A National Program for Library and Information Services: Proposals for Action." That is exactly what it is going to be. It is based on the need and the concept of sharing, cooperation. However, I think it is important to point out that cooperation is the most talked about term there is and the least understood and the least practiced.

Everybody defines cooperation as: What can you do for me? That is not cooperation. Cooperation is: What can I do for you? And until we get that attitude in the minds of librarians, administrators, legislators, people who work for the Bureau of the Budget or any place else, it is never going to work. You do not begin by saying: How do I save money? That is the way to waste money. You don't do a good budget by saying: How do I save money?

You begin the other way and you say: What are my goals? What am I trying to achieve? How am I going to achieve it? You develop objectives. How do I build an evaluation? How do I design it? Is it long range, and what do I mean by long range?

What are the short-range goals? How do I make sure? I am constantly checking to see how I am doing, and then what does it cost?

Once you have determined what it is going to cost, you must then look and see what dollars you have got, and if the dollars don't match what you need, then you do some trimming, but you do some trimming from an existing plan that has some logic to it, and you can still maintain your objectives. Maybe slow up some, or maybe take some of the frills off, but you must begin the other way, not with the dollars.

I never say to my staff, for example: Give me a budget for your department of $10,000.00 or $2.00. Never. Tell me what it is you need, and why you need it. Prove your case, in other words. Then, based upon that, I will do my budget, and then I have got to be able to defend that budget in the same way with my own boss and everybody else.

So that is the approach.

When I hear people say "I am going to save money," I only wish that you would avoid that concept and look at the other, and if you do the other right, you will, in fact, have better service and perhaps save money, or at least slow the rate of increase. That is the hope. Cooperatives will not save money, believe me, because you must buy staff time and all sorts of things. What they will do is slow the rate of increase, and cooperation is inevitable.

We have been studying library statistics for years, and we have been trying to come up with measures for evaluating library services, but nobody has been able to do so. None of the disciplines, including the library profession, has been able to do that.

Circulation statistics are the most criticized of all for being invalid and inaccurate. However, they are still among the few we have that we can easily handle, so we have got to use them, but we can't abuse them.

A local library, be it academic, school, public, or private, it doesn't matter, must have a certain level of resources, human as well as books. Only then can it be a worthy part of a network. You cannot be a parasite in the network.

For example, recently in Illinois Northwestern closed its doors to nonstudents. You must pay a fee to use Northwestern because they had so many students coming from the surrounding colleges which were poorly supported that they were serving the outsiders more than they were their own students, and after all, the money they were getting was for their students.

Now this is where federal and state governments come in. Federal and state governments recognize that in sharing resources you are going to have to take the weaker institutions, those that have a more limited responsibility, and somehow let them plug in to the other ones who have the resources and development over the years.

We have to be able to tap into the Library of Congress and Harvard and Yale. Of our 2,600 academic libraries, less than 100 are ARL members, really big libraries.

So in Illinois, for example, we pay on a cost basis certain resource centers to help supply the needs of institutions that can't do it themselves because they must cross institutional lines. The federal government must do so when they cross state lines.

So what you develop is a partnership of funding. You have a level of local funding which is essential to maintain the basic levels of service that institutions must provide. You then go to your state. You have to go beyond your local level because that is no longer the local government's responsibility, and when you go beyond the state, it becomes the federal government's responsibility.

With the property tax not being very good for public libraries and schools, for example, the obvious need at the state and federal level for funding for institutions and schools and libraries as well is absolutely essential. What the Commission is trying to do then in the totality of its report is to say: Here are the problems. We must share resources. We must use the best of technology and make suggestions on how to do that.

The cooperatives will only work if they are supported well by the nodes at the bottom. First the local, then the state, and then the federal. They will only work if there is a total integration of funding of services and resources.

We must become better managers. We must take advantage of computers and management systems to help us do our job. But don't forget. It is a very complex problem we have been dealing with for years.

There really hasn't been a new—if you will pardon me—a new thing said today. You go back and read library literature from 1876 on. You will find that almost everything we have said has been said before, and our job is to try to do better each year.

MODERATOR: Thank you, Al. Let me say in passing that the loafers you suggested the library systems of the country are serving are generally regarded by politicians as being people in the universities.

But let's now turn to questions and comments from the floor. Corrections of the panelists are in order. You may take them to task for not sticking to the subject that is advertised, or say anything you care to.

MR. ELLSWORTH MASON: I hate to go against the trends of this conference, but I would like to contend that bigger is better.

I grew up in the Yale University Library when it was one of the four greatest academic libraries in the world in the late 1940s, an eminence it no longer enjoys. I worked for eighteen months on a dissertation on Joyce which spread to practically every realm of knowledge, and I never once looked up anything that they did not have. I found materials that, had they not been present, I could not have obtained by interlibrary loan. I came across a number of very critical bits of information that led me in new directions in developing my intellectual program.

Now having said that, we ought to recognize too that our standards of living will be declining, in all aspects of our life, for some time to come. In our enthusiasm for new directions in librarianship, we are likely to get the idea that things we do for the sake of economy are good in themselves, but they are not necessarily so.

I think our strategy should be to fight the most skillful rear-guard action in just this way, putting the money that we have to the best possible use at every given level, and hoping that some day we will be able to turn things around. But I don't think the idea of shrinking to the absolutely bare minimal predictable use point, which is a trend that we are all being overtaken by, is in itself a good thing. I think we ought to make that very plain, because many of the bigger collections that do exist are in fact better.

PARTICIPANT (from Illinois): I would like to address the problem of periodicals and ask Al Trezza a question.

Some years ago I visited the National Lending Library for periodicals and was very much impressed with what they are doing in England. It is a small country, and the mail system is better, but they serve the university community and others in a very effective way.

I also became acquainted with the efforts which Dan Martin and the Associated Colleges of the Midwest are making in the development of their periodical bank, primarily for their own colleges but now for others as well.

I work for a consortium of the Big Ten Universities and the University of Chicago. These big libraries subscribe to anywhere from 20,000 to nearly 100,000 serials. The statistics on the use of these journals which I have heard at this conference and at other library conferences as well show that a relatively small portion of these vast hordes of journals are much used. Indeed, the universal experience of the National Lending Library and the ACM Periodical Bank is that the periodicals that everyone subscribes to are the ones that are called on the most.

Now the Center for Research Libraries, from reports I have been receiving, is moving more actively into this same area.

I understand from what I have heard earlier this week that their board or their constituency had agreed that the Center will be sort of a backup organization for all periodicals in science, technology, and the social sciences, and they have an arrangement with the British National Lending Library under which anything they cannot supply in Chicago, they will Telex across the Atlantic and a photocopy will be mailed that day or the next day.

Now has the National Commission been considering this problem? Can you tell us something about where it is going in this area?

MR. ALPHONSE TREZZA: The National Commission, in cooperation with the Association of Research Libraries, for the last three years has had a number of studies made, and one of them is called "Resources and Bibliographic Support of National Regional Centers" and another is "Access to Periodicals." Those are not the exact titles, but they cover the point.

One question we are asking is, Can we have a single periodical bank for the whole country? The general feeling seems to be that we are not sure that we can do what England did, because they are really a lot smaller in population and everything else. So we don't think a single bank is going to work for the United States.

However, we do think we need a National Periodical Resource Center which will be tied into regional centers on what they call a protocol or hierarchical basis. In other words, you still have to start at home, and utilize your state resources before you go bouncing off to the national. At least, we think that is the way it is going to go.

With monographs, it is even more so. We are convinced that it can't be a single national center. There will be a series of regional ones which will be tied together with, hopefully, the backup in Washington, say, of the Library of Congress.

So we are definitely working on both of these elements. In fact, we are in the process of setting up two task forces to try to move immediately on both tracks, but the point I make, and I want to make it again, is that you cannot use these centers as a crutch. You can use them as a supplement. Otherwise, the system will fall of its own weight.

Now we need some experience. We may find that after three or four or five years we can do a lot more cutting than we thought when we started, and that is fine. Then you have documentation, experiment, and research to prove it, and nobody can quarrel if you can give them the facts.

I want to end by saying that I too am a taxpayer, and I feel that the best use of my dollar is for education, which includes libraries, and if I had to make a choice between my dollar going for certain kinds of defense and ecological and energy programs, I would want it to go to education first.

MR. RAY HEFFNER: I think that there is a very definite place for these regional and national periodical banks in libraries, and I am delighted to see this effort proceeding, but I want to mention that I think there is going to be some other amelioration of the problem in the future.

Many of these scholarly periodicals are subsidized by academic budgets, and they are going to go under. Moreover, those that aren't subsidized depend heavily on library and individual purchasers; individuals don't have the money, and libraries don't either.

I think there is going to be a vast decrease in the number of low-utilization publications very shortly, and it is going to be very bad because some of the material that we need to have available will not be there.

There are all kinds of suggestions that one could make for a different distribution system. Eugene Garfield suggested that in some cases more people read an article before publication than afterwards, in the process of review and consideration by editors and so on. I think that is very well possible.

Why don't we have that review process, then publish a list with maybe an abstract of the articles, and say: Write to the author, and he will send you a Xerox copy. You probably would just get enough response to warrant what Dr. Garfield would like to do.

I was interested in Marvin Scilken's idea of buying cards for the catalog before the books, and then if there is enough demand, you go out and buy the books.

Why not carry that idea one step forward and ask the readers what they want to have written before the things get into print, and then we would only write those things for which there is sufficient demand as demonstrated in certain statistics. Wouldn't we all be better off?

PARTICIPANT (from Florida): I suppose everybody in the room is familiar with the draft standards for college libraries published in December by ACRL. What is the individual or the collective opinion of the panel with respect to the validity of those collection standards?

MR. ALPHONSE TREZZA: I think it is important to keep in mind that measurable standards are essential, at least in my experience. When I have gone to the legislature, whether it has been in Springfield or in Washington, and talked about library needs and money, they have wanted some specific figures. They want to know. You can't tell them you require a "quality collection."

They will say, "What does that mean?" And we librarians have been fighting for years to do away with quantitative standards. We maintain that quantitative standards tend to depreciate quality. You are just playing the numbers game, but, fortunately or unfortunately, it depends on the way you look at it, the budget people and the legislature say, "That is not good enough. What do you mean by quality? You have to give us a handle."

It is a big problem. You can argue whether standards are realistic or not, whether they are practical or not, but I don't think that you can argue for doing away with quantitative standards per se. But you cannot abuse them by making them a numbers game.

PARTICIPANT (from California): On the matter of accreditation, both Al and I have worked together on this when we were at ALA. We are aware of both the quantitative and the qualitative approach, but there is something to be said for both aspects of this.

Now Mr. Semrow, you were speaking of the move away from the quantitative, and having been very active in accreditation, I have always looked with some consternation at the focus on quantitative measures. But now as a library administrator, I just thank the good Lord that we had some quantitative approach because the action of ALA at midwinter saved us. The specification of 6 percent of the general and educational budget as the required minimum for the library was a very fine indicator, though not ideal. But certainly we need a statement to the effect that any library with less than 6 percent could certainly not function effectively.

MODERATOR: I must wonder aloud whether, if each component of the university were to present the president with the minimum effective percentage of budget with which they could operate, would the total percentage exceed a hundred?

Are there other questions?

MR. JOSEPH SEMROW: I would like to say that I would agree, along with Mr. Trezza, that it is helpful to have some benchmarks. He spoke about the abuse of such things, and that is one of the things we have to keep in mind.

Many institutions that are under development frequently write in to us and ask: What standards do you have for this? What standards do you have for that? And I frequently will send them the standards from the American Library Association, and so on, and suggest that they use these appropriately, and that they might be helpful as a starting point, as a reference point, but not as something that is an arbitrary standard to follow in every instance.

PARTICIPANT (from New York State): I have been very stimulated by this conference, and congratulate you on pulling it together, but I am concerned by what seems to be an underlying lack or a weakness, at least in my perception.

The emphasis in the titles of the papers and the remarks was on limited or zero collection growth. It seems to me that there should be a shared responsibility to insure that there is nonetheless adequate access.

I think this has been said, but not said adequately, that while we proceed to limit or talk about the way to limit growth within institutions, somehow we have got to acknowledge that it is not only the state's, but our own, responsibility to find or to build up better the mechanisms that make it possible to improve access to resources.

I think that colleges are presently taking advantage of such mechanisms, and it is my opinion that that was underemphasized in the remarks.

MR. ALPHONSE TREZZA: I would like to put on my political hat, if you don't mind, from both the federal and state levels and tell you that one of the most devastating things that you can do is to use that term "no growth." That is a bad term because it would be misunderstood and misused against you.

What you are talking about is the intelligent use of your funds. That is what you want to argue about. That is what we have been saying for the last two days. We haven't been saying negatively: Stop the library from growing. What we are asking is: How do we do a better job with our funds? And how do we communicate that book selection is both adding and weeding, and that the two things are part of the whole?

So let's watch the terms that we use. The budget people may misunderstand, and they will then set arbitrary limits and say: You can only have 10,000 volumes.

Many years ago we were planning a building for a college library in Pennsylvania, and we were arguing then: What is the right size for a college library? We seized on 60,000 books. Within three years they were planning the undergraduate library at Harvard, and they ended up by saying: No, it was 100,000. Northwestern has that core collection that doesn't circulate. That is 100,000 volumes. So what is the right number? Be careful when you arbitrarily say that the core collection, or whatever it is, is this number or that number. You can approximate, but don't get yourselves hung up on specifics of this kind because politically we have enough problems fighting for our money now.

I was told last week, when I was in Washington and talked to the Minority Leader's legislative aide about library programs, "You realize, of course, today, that with Viet Nam and Cambodia and the Middle East and the energy crisis and the economy and all, you know libraries are fifteenth priority," and I said, "No way. No way." I said,

"We are first." I said, "If you gave us first priority, maybe we wouldn't have some of these problems. Maybe we could educate people to solve these problems. That is your trouble. You have misplaced your priority."

What I am saying is that you had better believe in what you do. Otherwise, leave the profession and go join the budget cutters.

MR. DANIEL GORE: Ordinarily I am very bashful about speaking up in public, especially on warm issues, but I do want to answer the criticism raised by the gentleman who spoke before Mr. Trezza because I think he has an excellent point.

There has been little said at this conference, at least not as much as I had hoped, regarding the possibilities of considerably increasing the performance rate of libraries while keeping their size constant. You are quite right. Not much has been said about this. Dick Trueswell did talk about it. Mike Buckland talked about it somewhat. They both touched on it rather tangentially. I think they may have assumed that everyone in this audience has followed their work with the same degree of interest and admiration as I have.

But out of the concerns of the sort that Mike Buckland and the research team at Lancaster have been investigating, out of the sort of inventory phenomena that Dick Trueswell has been investigating, have in fact come, I believe, for the first time, measures of performance of libraries of a kind that we have never considered before. Instead of saying, "My library has a million volumes, therefore it is better than this library that has a half million," we ask the question: What percentage of the demand made on your collection by your patrons can you meet? And people like Buckland and Trueswell have discovered effective, economical techniques for making such measurements.

Mr. Buckland found at the University of Lancaster, for example, that the availability rate of books owned by his library, around 1967, was at a level of about 60 percent. They took the interesting measure of reducing the loan period for high-demand items from a full semester to something like a week. The result was that the availability rate jumped from 60 to 86 percent. That could be measured.

And when that happened, the per capita circulation rate nearly doubled. Service was improved, and people started using that library.

But I am glad you raised this question. I think perhaps we could have another conference some day on just this one issue of improving performance. For these things are very closely related, and the idea of maintaining a no-growth collection is not one simply of saving money.

It is one of spending your money in such a way that you get the best possible return from it, and what Trueswell, Buckland, and many others are finding is that we can get just a hell of a lot more service out of our libraries for the same money we are now spending, or even less.

MODERATOR: As a layman in the library field, I want to say that I have been puzzled by the antagonism and the downright insults provoked by the Periodical Bank's discovery of the enormous unmet need for commonly held periodicals. This attitude, that if the card is in the catalog, then everybody who wants the item has access to it, from my point of view as a consumer simply won't do.

PARTICIPANT (from New York State): I quite agree with Mr. Gore, as another student of the strategies posed by Mr. Buckland, that these are very important, and we need to encourage more use of them. But I think we still haven't emphasized your responsibility and my responsibility to share the resources of our own libraries, wherever we decide to make the cutoff point in our own collections.

MR. MARVIN SCILKEN: When we try to develop networks, I hope we will not do that as a way to bail out rich towns at the expense of poor towns such as the one I serve. In our area two or three of the wealthiest cities pay the least proportionately for membership in a library network. Yet they make big use of the network.

Have you done any work to assure that it is not going to be another inverse Robin Hood principle at work here, to see that we are not ripped off any further by the rich, Mr. Trezza?

MR. ALPHONSE TREZZA: We are going to have to depend on you out there to make sure that it doesn't happen.

MR. MARVIN SCILKEN: We have to depend on you because it happens just like that.

MODERATOR: We have not only the poor with us in academic libraries, but also the undergraduates.

MR. RAY HEFFNER: What Mr. Scilken has just said illustrates something that has been worrying me in this whole conference. There is too much emphasis on what percentage of the existing demand do we satisfy. Maybe there is demand that *should* exist but doesn't, whether it's a college or whether it's a community.

I think we may need some affirmative action programs. You know, the program doesn't say to you that it is sufficient to open your doors to minority students and members of the majority sex. It is important to get out there and do something actively about it.

I think, of course, I am not as obstreperous as I sound. But I don't think we can tie library development entirely to the satisfaction of the very current set of demands. We will have a very inadequate service to the kinds of publics, several of them, that we ought to be serving more effectively. So I was glad to hear your emphasis on this point.

MODERATOR: I agree that is an important consideration, and it leads us even further away from current acquisitions policies.

PARTICIPANT (from Minnesota): On the same topic, it was mentioned that, of the 2,600 academic libraries, there are 100 major resource libraries. That is true, but there are a large number of small libraries that in reality are the libraries' last resort.

There are a lot of small libraries that have collections that Harvard and Yale do not have and will never have. I think that there has to be some type of recognition of these libraries and some type of support in terms of what they are keeping.

If I took our library, and followed the measures that we have been discussing in terms of what to throw out, there would be, for one thing, probably 40,000 manuscripts on microfilm that wouldn't be available.*

But there are other factors that have to be looked at. I don't think they are being looked at in this conference as sharply as they should.

MR. ALPHONSE TREZZA: I would like to say, for example, that I would not judge my library on the measures that were suggested by Buckland and the others. That is not enough.

When I was at the University of Pennsylvania, I was head of Circulation. I know about records. We had more in-library use than we had circulation. Buckland completely ignores it. Maybe it will fit the circulation curve beautifully, but until we know that, I won't accept just half of the solution.

MR. MICHAEL BUCKLAND: I just want to make a point that at the University of Lancaster we do, in fact, try to measure in-library use as well as recorded circulation.

MR. ALPHONSE TREZZA: But the figures that we got were just on the one thing, which is great, but it is only half of the thing.

PARTICIPANT : What technique do you use?

MR. MICHAEL BUCKLAND: Every three months or so, we try to

*Editor's note: None of the measures proposed in the conference papers is intended to apply to archival collections such as the microfilmed manuscripts mentioned here.

put signal papers in books so that we can tell if they were used, and we also look at reshelving and special return boxes.

PARTICIPANT (from Massachusetts): I would like to speak on behalf of taking affirmative action. Those of us who are in the selection process have selected material that we doubted had acute, immediate demand, not because we felt that this material will be needed, but that our clientele should be exposed to it. We have taken affirmative action by improving reference services and other public services and by leading the user to the materials we have purchased. We have thereby met some economic concerns by making better use of what we have purchased.

PARTICIPANT (from California): I think there is no question as to the merit of this conference from the standpoint of exposure to new ideas. One of the things that continues to concern me, though, is that if we go to the extreme in these theories—and I am not unmindful of your arguments on duplicating in quantity those things that are used, rather than spending money on things that are not used—what concerns me is that we are too rapidly becoming an Orwellian Society. And I can see in the small liberal arts colleges people exposed only to quantities of books that have been assigned without ever experiencing serendipity and the opening of their consciousness to creative and stimulating things that in the long run we may very well need in our society.

MODERATOR: Are there other comments?

PARTICIPANT (from Pennsylvania): I think it was a pity that Dick Trueswell's talk this morning didn't reiterate* one of the points he made in an earlier paper, that the statistical analysis he was doing did not replace the decision the library has to make. It provided an additional tool, and I think that anybody who suggests or thinks that the people who are working on statistical methods regard these as anything but a tool to assist in decision-making, and not to replace the decision, goes away with quite an erroneous view of people doing operations research within libraries. One or two people have indicated in their remarks that that was being advocated—that statistics replace decisions. They do not. All they do is give you a tool.

PARTICIPANT (from Missouri): One thing we have talked about for the last two days as a possible solution to space problems has been cooperative storage facilities. The University of Missouri is actively

*Editor's note: It did.

considering building such a facility, and one of the considerations that I think we haven't realistically come up against, which the panel can address, has to do with accreditation.

We have a system with four campuses at St. Louis, Kansas City, Rolla, and Columbia, with very different libraries and very different-sized campuses. Each of them at the moment is barely meeting standards for its class of university.

Now if we put the "overflow materials" from these four campus libraries, which are barely meeting standards now, into one central storage facility, how will that be viewed by accrediting agencies, and against standards like those from ALA which say that you must have these things readily available to your users, when we are saying that we are taking these fractions away and making them less available? Is there attention paid in the standards as to how quickly and readily accessible materials need to be?

MR. RAY HEFFNER: Joe can answer this better, but the North Central Association, which is your regional accrediting association, does not have standards of that quantified sort.

As examiners, we go on to the campus, and we ask: What are your library resources? How readily are they available to those students and other users who need them? We look at the whole range, and we are just as interested in off-campus storage and the rapidity of access to those facilities as we are in how many books you have in your own building on your own campus.

There may still be some benighted professional accrediting associations that retain rigid quantifiable standards, but I doubt they are still as rigid as the myth suggests they are. So if you keep the question of access in mind, if you keep in mind the whole range of questions that have been raised in these two days, you have no problems on accreditation.

MR. JOSEPH SEMROW: The test would be really, I suspect, what the accrediting teams find. They get some students together and say: Can you get these books that you need? Where are they? And so on. Are they available to you? And if the answer is "yes," of course, it means one thing, and if it is "no," it means other things. So that is really where the test is. Are the books satisfactorily available to the students? Not where are they stored and in what quantities.

MODERATOR: It sounds like quite a subversive position for the accrediting associations to take. Let us hope that message does get out, and that every librarian who has told his academic vice-president that accreditation will be lost if a certain percentage were not spent on the library, bites his tongue.

PARTICIPANT (from West Virginia): There was a lot of talk about objectives, that you couldn't start measuring, that you couldn't decide what to discard until you talked about the objectives of the library.

My question to Mr. Semrow concerns the official stand of the accrediting agencies, that they don't tell an institution what its objectives should be. They just try and tell the institutions how well they are meeting their objectives. Is that a fair statement?

MR. JOSEPH SEMROW: The institutions say, "We are meeting our objectives thus and so," and then the task of the team is to go to the campus and, through self-study and their conferences and interviews with faculty, administrators, and students, they verify this.

PARTICIPANT (from West Virginia): State budget offices across the nation are coming up with very specific formulas for funding institutions, and they don't really ask the institutions what their mission is. They just say: This is the formula by which we generate your funds, in one way or another. The accrediting agencies don't ask the institution whether their mission is wrong, as you said, in your response to my question. In view of the retrenchment in higher education, do you think that the accrediting agencies may come around to the point of saying that your goals or your mission, as you have stated them, are unrealistic?

MR. JOSEPH SEMROW: I think there is a certain point at which a team might question an institution's statement of mission, but I don't think it is in this particular regard.

I agree with the view set forth by Mr. Trezza that, in terms of higher education as a social enterprise, we have to set our goals for that and help set the priorities of our society, and see that we move toward them and do what we can to get the priorities set properly.

Now with respect to such things as state funding formulas, we have come up against these in a number of cases, and I would say probably on principle that a very different view is taken of such formulas per se, because usually they turn out to be applied appropriately, but this is a great problem. It is a problem of state coordinating boards and such agencies, and it is one which we are just getting into.

MODERATOR: Very often the formula itself comes more from the state coordinating commission or board than from a budget agency, so the coordinating board would be selling it to the budget agency and the governor and cramming it down the throat of the institutions.

MR. RAY HEFFNER: We would not say—at least I wouldn't as a member of an accrediting team: Your goals are perhaps wrong. But we might very well, and often do, say: The probability of your getting adequate support to meet those goals seems low.

PARTICIPANT (from West Virginia): There is an unreality here somewhere, whether it is at the institution or the state level.

MODERATOR: Certainly what Joe mentioned at the outset about the very sharp increase in the number of institutions in the North Central area that offer doctoral degrees may partially explain where the unreality arises.

MR. JOSEPH SEMROW: In the situation Ray just described, a team has to make a recommendation that on the basis of apparently inadequate funding this situation will not be accredited, and then put it right to the state to come back with a response.

MODERATOR: Certainly a good many Chambers of Commerce in university towns have been persuaded to tell their legislators that, unless a Ph.D. program is started at University X, we simply are not going to be able to attract any decent faculty. That canard has been uttered with scandalous frequency.

MR. ALPHONSE TREZZA: I want to make one comment just to correct a wrong impression. I think that the studies we've heard about here, and I have read about the Buckland studies and the Trueswell studies and all the others, are absolutely very important.

I have been involved with library statistics for years, and I don't want in any way to have anybody misunderstand me. Statistics are essential to our decision-making.

All I am saying is that we must now go all the way. Take the Lancaster study, for example, on in-house use, and let's see whether we can come up with some more figures there to give us a total formula. So don't go away thinking that I don't believe these are significant studies presented at this conference. They certainly are.

Daniel Gore

"All the rivers run into the sea;
yet the sea is not full."
—ECCLESIASTES 1:7

Farewell to Alexandria: The Theory of the No-Growth, High-Performance Library

When Abraham Lincoln was asked how long a man's legs should be, he replied "Long enough to reach the ground." One feels confortable with such an answer: it makes sense, it conforms to reality, it doesn't strain the imagination.

When one asks a librarian how large a library should be, the invariable answer is "Larger. And with provision for further expansion fifteen years hence." One used to feel comfortable with that answer too, because it made sense of a sort (at least to academicians, who intuitively know there is no such thing as enough books). It certainly conformed to the only reality we have known since the foundation of the Alexandrian Library 2,300 years ago. Libraries have always grown until fire, flood, or fighting put an end to them.

But lately the answer has begun to weigh upon the imagination—at least of those who pause to reflect upon the consequences of the observed geometric growth rate of academic libraries in the twentieth century.

For several decades now, academic library collections have been doubling every fifteen years or so. University libraries that held several hundred thousand volumes in the 1930s hold several million today. At that rate, many of them would become, in just fifty more years, about the size of the Library of Congress—a library of such gargantuan dimensions that it calls upon the resources of a whole nation to sustain it.

The budgets of some present-day university libraries exceed the total institutional budgets of some small colleges. Yet, some of those colleges have libraries whose growth rates will, if maintained over the next fifty years, bring them up to the multimillion-volume levels of the great university libraries.

Is anyone prepared to believe that the nation will ever suport a hundred university libraries the size of today's Library of Congress, whose annual budget is approaching a hundred million dollars? Or that colleges fifty years hence will be able to devote to their libraries the constant-dollar equivalent of their current total institutional budget?

The imagination recoils from such absurd visions. One turns away from this problem, as from so many others, with the soothing conviction that the next generation will surely solve it, especially since they will have the benefit of four times as many books as we have today to guide them in their thinking.

A dilemma arises here, for the library buildings we have today will not hold four times their present content. Most of them are already full, or soon will be, in spite of the fact that the last eight years (1967-1974) witnessed the biggest building boom in library history. But it failed to solve the space problem. Although new space was created for 163 million more volumes, 166 million were added to collections in the boom years, thus making the space problem today a little worse than when the boom began.

The boom is over, and building growth is falling rapidly behind collection growth, with prospects for new building money becoming ever more bleak. So the problem of coping with the geometric growth of academic libraries just will not wait for the next generation to solve it. We will have to solve it for them, and not by adding more space. We tried that, and it did not work.

One other solution that has been tried, and also proved a failure, is miniaturization, through microfilming or computer storage or any other technique. While certain results are achieved by those measures—for example, vast and probably useless expansion of total resources and reduction of data-retrieval times—they contribute nothing to the solution of the physical growth problem. The highest growth rates in the history of academic libraries have occurred precisely during the thirty-year period when microtechnology was on the ascendant. Microtechnology has had no effect on the space problem, partially because librarians typically acquire publications in microformat *only* when, for whatever reason, they cannot or will not acquire them on paper. Microform collections have thus generally developed not as substitutes for something bulkier, but as collections that simpply would not have existed in any form had they not been available in microform. (The use that is actually made of general microform collections is notoriously low, so low that one suspects that in most cases far more economical methods could be provided for delivering their content to a patron, if and when the demand arose. Replacing journal backruns with micro-equivalents, for example, is in most instances economic folly. Demand on most journal backruns in nearly all libraries is so near zero that one should simply remove them, perhaps to some regional lending center, and be done with them completely.)

The solution to the growth problem will be found, I believe, not in the development of new technology to shore up the cracking foundations of the ever-climbing Tower of Babel, but in thinking carefully about that most perplexing question, How large should a library be?

Such answers as have been given fall into three categories, which I call the Alexandrian, the Philosophical, and the Scientific. I will analyze each of them separately, starting with the Alexandrian because it represents the first effort in history to determine the proper size of a library; and because, as will be seen later, the Philosophical and Scientific answers, while coming 2,000 years after the Alexandrian, are in fact merely subspecies of it, tricked out to look like something genuinely modern and original.

The Alexandrian, or heroic-impulsive, answer to the question, How large should a library be? arose with the formation of the Alexandrian Library in 300 B.C., almost coincidentally with the origin of the distinctive Western attitude that bigger means better and that limits are inherently bad. The Alexandrian answer is that a library should acquire everything it possibly can and keep it forever, lest something of inestimable value perish from the earth through negligence or misvaluation.

Since that idea still dominates and pervades academic librarianship after 2,300 years, I want to dwell at some length on the founding, flourishing, and ultimate destruction of the Alexandrian Library, which first planted the seed whence our present difficulties sprang. By speculating at leisure on the motives and methods of those old librarians, we may understand a little better what it is that prompts us to imitate their objectives and what the outcome of that imitation is likely to be.

Founded around 300 B.C. in the city of Alexandria, in Egypt, by

Ptolemy Soter or his son Ptolemy Philadelphus, the library grew in ten years to a size of some 200,000 volumes (so says Josephus the Jewish historian). Aulus Gellius and Ammianus Marcellinus both attest it had reached a size of 700,000 volumes by the year 47 B.C., when the harbor of Alexandria was fired by Julius Caesar and a portion of the library burned, according to disputed testimony.[1]

Over a period of some 250 years, it appears that this far-famed library had grown at an average rate of some 3,000 volumes per year. This in an era when there were neither publishing houses nor printing presses to multiply books in the prodigious quantities to which we are accustomed today. More than 2,000 years would pass before any other library would attain the astonishing size of the Alexandrian. Even in the 250 years following Gutenberg's invention of the art of printing from movable type, not a single library grew to the size reached by the Alexandrian in its first 250 years.

How did these transplanted Greeks, in an Egyptian city founded by the Macedonian menace, bring so many books together in so little time? Their first step was to form what is called the Museum, but more properly a University, and induce the brightest ornaments of Greek learning and arts to serve on its faculty.

Among that mighty stream of intellectuals that flowed into Alexandria, at the bidding of the Ptolemies, were Euclid the geometrician, Herophilus the anatomist, the philosophers Theodorus, Strato, Diodorus the Carian, and Hegesias of Cyrene, the poet Callimachus and the playwright Philemon, and Eratosthenes the polymath, who was mathematician, geographer, astronomer, grammarian, chronographer, historian, philologist, philosopher, and poet besides, all rolled into one. (We might call him one of the earliest interdisciplinary majors—an entire faculty under one hat.)

Naturally, such men would employ themselves in reading and writing many books—the more so since it appears that none of them had to offer so much as one hour of class instruction per semester—and a library is as necessary for them as music is for dancers. Being a faculty, they would certainly want to order as many books as possible for the library, and Ptolemy provided unlimited book budgets for them. He also provided a library director for them, making one out of Demetrios of Phaleron, a scholarly sort who had recently been banished from Athens, where he had ruled as regent under the Macedonians for a decade, until he was overthrown by another Demetrius, son of Antigonus.

Demetrios achieved some notoriety for his personal elegance and the sumptuousness of his entertaining, at least before he became a library director, but his latter end was worse than his beginning. After ten years' service as Ptolemy's chief librarian and trusted personal adviser, he made the mistake of recommending the wrong royal son as Ptolemy's successor. Ptolemy chose another son; and when he, Ptolemy II (called Philadelphus) came into power, he promptly sacked Demetrios and banished him to Busiris (Upper Egypt), where afterwards, says Laertius, "Somehow, in his sleep he received an asp-bite," and died. History furnishes no other record of a librarian sleeping with an asp.

Back to the library: How did Demetrios and his successors amass that 700,000-volume collection over the library's first 250 years? Their main object was to collect the whole corpus of extant Greek literature and produce authoritative editions, calling on their illustrious scholarly staff for the editorial work and their own scribes for the copying. In this respect, the library combined the functions of a present-day publishing house, printing press, and library all under one roof.

Galen tells how, under Ptolemy III (Euergetes), autograph or otherwise authentic manuscripts of Aeschylus, Sophocles, and Euripedes were borrowed from Athens, a deposit of fifteen talents being made against their safe return. The deposit was, of course, forfeited, and the librarians of Alexandria added yet another unique treasure to their holdings.

Wanting a library copy of the Hebrew Old Testament in a fashionable tongue, Demetrios engaged seventy-two Jewish scholars to translate it into Greek. Afterwards, the translation became known as the Septuagint, literally "The Seventy."

The librarians also appear to have collected and translated Egyptian texts and anything else they could get their hands on.

Ships making port in Alexandria were searched for manuscripts. When found, they were confiscated by the library, copies were made and delivered to the luckless owners, and the originals were added to the library's collections.

By far the largest single acquisition occurred when Mark Antony stole the famous rival library of Pergamum and gave the whole thing—200,000 volumes— to Cleopatra as a love token. Having nothing better to do with it at the time, she turned it over to the Alexandrian Library for safekeeping, until she should need it. Had the

Alexandrians only known two centuries earlier how things would turn out, maybe they would not have jealously embargoed the shipment of papyrus to Pergamum, to frustrate Eumenes II's ambition to build there a library surpassing the Alexandrian. Their jealousy of the library at Pergamum deserves special attention because it affords a clear and reliable glimpse of the real motives underlying their collection-development policies.

While we know a good deal about *how* the Alexandrian scholar/librarians went about forming their mammoth collection, so far as I can tell nobody has ever ventured to ask *why* they did it—at least on such a stupendous scale. That tells you something about the potency and pervasiveness of the Alexandrian model, when, over a stretch of 2,300 years, nobody even dares ask what was the sense of the thing. (I have noticed that scholars are fond of urging everybody to inquire closely into the *reasons* of things, unless it happens to be something the scholars themselves are doing.)

My personal notion of why the Alexandrian Greeks built their library on such a Heraclean scale is summed up in the adjective I have just used: *Heraclean.* For the Alexandrian Library strikes me as the ultimate expression of Greek narcissism in institutional form: heroic in scope, jealous of all rivals, never satisfied with present triumphs, but always driven to seek fresh and more dazzling ones, an institution gone out of control and essentially mindless. It is the precise institutional analogue of the mythical Heracles, the Greek archetype of the hero, whose narcissistic folly Philip Slater, the anthropologist, regards as typical of the pathological narcissism of Greek society in general. (For more on that intriguing subject, see Slater's ironically titled book *The Glory of Hera*, published in 1968 by Beacon Press.)

What became of that enormous collection of books the Alexandrians put together over the centuries?

The Christians say the Romans destroyed it (in 47 B.C.), and the Moslems say the Christians destroyed it (in 391 A.D.). And some historians say that the Moslems destroyed whatever was left of it when they seized Alexandria in 646 A.D. Parsons believes that a great deal was left, arguing that neither the Romans nor the Christians accounted for more than a fraction of the total loss.

The legend of the Moslem destruction goes like this. One 'Amr ibn al 'As wrote to the Caliph 'Umar b. al Khattāb, asking what should be done with all the books in that marvelous library. Being something of a logician, the Caliph replied, "As for the books you mention, if their contents agree with the Book of God, then having the Book of God we are wealthy without them; and if they contradict the Book of God we have no need of them, so start destroying them." Which 'Amr ibn al 'As did, distributing them throughout the city to be burned either in baths or fireplaces, whichever tradition you prefer to believe. To me a bath has always seemed an unusual place for a fire, but when you consider what they were burning, so is a fireplace. For by the seventh century A.D. the bulk of a library would consist of parchment scrolls or codices, and parchment is not flammable.

My own theory is that the citizens of Alexandria periodically disposed of major portions of their rapidly growing library themselves, panicking at the realization that it might otherwise eventually push them all into the sea. I like to think they hung onto the precious Greek literary heritage, removing only the encrustations of scholarship that enveloped it over the centuries—the hundreds of thousands of theses, dissertations, exegetical, critical, and other epiphytic works that flourished upon the infinitely smaller corpus of real Greek literature.

We have pretty clear evidence that the Alexandrian Library experienced acute space problems early in its history. For by the time of Callimachus's death around 235 B.C., a branch library of considerable size had been created in the Serapeum, in a separate quarter of the city. Its holdings are variously estimated at between 100,000 and 300,000 volumes. Now the first appearance of a branch research library in the same city, or on the same campus can mean only one thing: the main library has filled up, and, for the moment at least, the easiest escape from the embarrassment is to open a branch in another building. Then the branch fills up. That is when people begin to realize, as I think the Alexandrians did, that there will be no end of branches unless you periodically address yourself to the roots of the problem.

Whatever the cause of the Library's disappearance a thousand years after its founding, of the 700,000 or more volumes those ancient librarians collected and preserved, only some 500 works from classical antiquity have reached us more or less textually intact, not one of them being the actual copy originally held by the Alexandrian Library. Mostly it is wheat, not chaff, that survived, lending weight to my theory that the Alexandrian citizenry disposed of the superfluous portions of their collections themselves. Had the librarians been allowed to have their way, Egypt today would be an occupied country—every square foot of its surface occupied by the Alexandrian Library.

Rarely do libraries play a significant role in the long-term survival of books. In short-term preservation, yes; long-term survival, no. The Bible exists today not because librarians preserved it for 2,000 years, but because scribes, and then printers, endlessly reproduced it.

Though the historical outcome of the Alexandrian approach to preservation is not reassuring, college and university faculties are instinctively Alexandrian in their view of the library. The sheer magnitude of numbers at least forces them to give up the idea of acquiring everything—50 million books published since Gutenberg; 400,000 new ones each year, plus some 300,000 new serials volumes. But nothing will persuade them to give up a volume once it has been acquired.

So much for the Alexandrian answer to the question, How large should a library be?

More recently, there has been the Philosophical answer, which stipulates that an academic library should be large enough to hold whatever books are needed to support the curriculum, to support research where graduate programs are conducted, and to permit some "recreational reading." The Philosophical answer has the merit of plausibility, but gives no clue as to the actual size of the library required, beyond the relative indication that a larger library will be required to support a "larger" curriculum. The Philosophical answer avoids any forthright mention of what will happen to the collection if, say, a segment of the curriculum is simply dropped, or course content is updated in such a way that much of the existing collection proves to be either irrelevant or erroneous. Proponents of the Philosophical view studiously avoid offending the Alexandrians by tacitly pretending that the reason for bringing a book into a library is also a reason for keeping it there forever. To pretend that is to pretend that the curriculum today is precisely that of the last century, although of course "larger." But one is tempted to pretend almost anything rather than risk the hissing cry of "Philistine!" from the Alexandrians who, while prepared to concede that a curriculum must change, and that courses once offered need not be offered forever, nonetheless insist that the library that "supports" the curriculum must forever be the same library, only larger. The Philosophical answer by default amounts to agreeing that an academic library shall always be larger. It is mere Alexandrianism in plausible disguise.

Finally, there is the Scientific answer, which has the virtue of providing exact numbers of volumes required, by means of a formula based on such variables as enrollment, size of faculty, and number of graduate fields. The principal value of the Scientific answer is that it may favorably impress a fiscal officer who is not disposed to pry too deeply into your bedrock scientific formula and discover that the whole thing miraculously floats upon a bottomless swamp of pure impressionism. It should be noted that the Scientific answer applies only to questions of "How small may a library properly be?" It is calculated to frighten administrators into believing their library is too small and is thus couched exclusively in terms of minimums. It resolutely ignores the question "How large should a library be?" as its proponents assume that anyone in his right mind knows a library should be just as big as it possibly can be and should always be growing bigger. The Scientific answer is pure narcissism, concealed in sober mathematical garb.

The Alexandrian, the Philosophical, and the Scientific approach to libraries all require that they always grow larger, world without end.[2] So potent and pervasive is this trinity, one would not dare speak out against it unless its ultimate outcome were both manifestly absurd and close at hand. Now that race car drivers are publicly declaring that speed limits are needed on the Indy 500, it may be permissible for a librarian to propose that size limits are needed for libraries.

If we put aside our Alexandrian prejudices for a moment and ask what is the main function of an academic library, rather than how large it should be, I think we will get general agreement that its primary function is to provide books[3] for readers who want to read them *now*. (No suggestion is intended that academic libraries have no proper archival or preservational role. Undoubtedly they do, but the proportion of their holdings devoted to that function is insignificant in relation to the space problem.) Though we may fret ourselves in a high-minded way about the imagined needs of our patrons in the twenty-first century, the needs we must actually fill are those of the patron standing on the other side of the circulation desk, plaintively asking to be told why *he* so rarely finds the books he needs to read. The answer usually has nothing to do with the size of the collection; or, rather, it is not because the collection is too small.

When we suspend the perplexing question of collection size and instead ask questions about performance rates in relation to necessary functions, some unexpected results ensue, one of them being that by making your collection smaller you can actually provide more and better service.

Let us first ask what is an acceptable performance rate with regard to recorded holdings. To an Alexandrian the required rate is 100 percent—that is, the library should own, and the catalog should record, every book that every patron, present or future, may ever ask for. To achieve that ideal rate you will have to own some 50 million books and add about 400,000 new ones every year, plus 300,000 new serial volumes.

If you will agree to a rate less than 100 percent, some surprising things happen. Several years ago, the Yale Library discovered it owned about 90 percent of the books its patrons wanted to see, yet it owned only 2,500,000 titles, or 5 percent of the total that might be asked for. By falling off the Alexandrian ideal a mere 10 percent, the Yale Library could forego the purchase of 47,500,000 books—and the construction of a library twice the size of the Empire State Building to hold them.

Consider now another measure of library performance: the availability rate, by which I mean the rate of success in finding on the shelves a book you want that the catalog says the library owns. Recent inquiries into this phenomenon indicate that an availability rate around 50 percent may be the norm. Assume now that you can find entries in the catalog for 90 percent of the books you want to see, and that you will find 50 percent of those actually on the shelves. The net result is a performance rate of 45 percent, which is dismal, but not because the library is too small. The cause lies elsewhere, and the remedy is not to add more titles to the collection.

During the 1960s, R. W. Trueswell, now chairman of the Industrial Engineering Department at the University of Massachusetts, published a series of statistical studies of library inventory phenomena showing that a very small proportion of an academic library's collection accounts for nearly all the use.[4] He makes the intriguing suggestion that 40 percent of a collection may account for 99 percent of the recorded use;[5] and, if that be so, then at least half the collection may be removed without perceptibly affecting the availability of books that people will actually read. Trueswell's astonishing predictions so offend the Alexandrian temperament that they have met with the most devastating possible response from the library profession: they have been ignored.

Corollary to the proposition that most books in a large library are rarely or never used is the proposition that a small percentage of books are always in very heavy demand and thus frequently unavailable when you want to borrow them. Hence, in most libraries you are likely to fail nearly half the time to find the book you want, though the library owns it. The demand is too heavy for the supply, and libraries usually give no systematic attention to the problem. One library that did—The University of Lancaster's—discovered that when measures were taken to improve the availability rate from 60 to 86 percent, by shortening the loan period of high-demand books, the per capita use rate more than doubled.[6] Had they instead doubled the number of titles in the collection, the availability rate would have been imperceptibly affected.

At the moment one can find very little data to answer these three essential questions regarding an academic library's performance:

(1) What percentage of books wanted by patrons are recorded in the catalog? (The Holdings Rate).

(2) What percentage of wanted books recorded in the catalog are available on the shelves? (The Availability Rate).

(3) What percentage of all books a patron wants are available to him on the shelves? (The Performance Rate: Holdings Rate times Availability Rate).

From the patron's standpoint the third question is the one that really matters. The librarian's problem is to decide what combination of Holdings and Availability Rates will yield the best results with the available resources.

Though scant, data now available on these matters are sufficient to make it worthwhile for any library to begin testing certain hypotheses aimed at improving Performance Rates while reducing collection size. I will present an illustration here to show what is realistically possible, using estimates which, though they certainly will not apply exactly to any one library's situation, should prove close enough to suggest a suitable point of departure.

Assume a university library with the following characteristics:

Collection size	1,000,000 vols.
Shelfload factor	100%
Current additions	50,000 vols./yr.
Enrollment	20,000 students
Holdings Rate	90%
Availability Rate	50%
Performance Rate	45%

The Performance Rate in this library is quite poor, but is probably typical of such libraries. A decision is made to improve it, by going the traditional route of adding to the holdings. Consider now the result that will be obtained by the most extreme imaginable application of the Alexandrian ideal: by some miracle you create a library holding every book under the sun, and add to it everything that is published everywhere as it comes off the press. Your library now holds 50 million volumes, and each year you add 700,000 new ones. Your Holdings Rate climbs to 100 percent, but your Availability Rate remains 50 percent, for you have done nothing to affect it. The Performance Rate (the product of Holdings and Availability Rates) thus moves up from 45 to 50 percent and, though you have spent two billion dollars on the project, your patrons perceive things to be far worse than they were before, because they now have to walk ten times as far to suffer about the same number of disappointments as before.

The tenure of university librarians over the last fifteen years parallels in brevity that of university presidents, because they sought to improve Performance Rates by zealously attending to Holdings Rates, while ignoring the availability problem. Nothing really happened, except that their libraries got bigger and they got another job.

Keeping in mind the Trueswell predictions regarding collection size and Holdings Rates, and the University of Lancaster's experience with Availability Rates, let us now consider how we may radically improve Performance Rates by drastically cutting collection size.

Using Trueswell's simple statistical criterion for predicting which books in the collection will receive little or no use in the future, we remove 300,000 of them at one fell swoop. The Holdings Rate now drops from 90 to 89 percent. Why so little? Because the Holdings Rate applies to books that people will want to read, and you have statistically contrived to leave practically all of those books in the library.

At the same time, by statistical methods we identify those books whose predictable demand is so great that one or more added copies will be needed to achieve a certain predictable Availability Rate. By computer simulation, we determine that 100,000 added copies will bring the Availability Rate to 95 percent, which is the best we can afford.

We now have a collection of 800,000 volumes, a Holdings Rate of 89 percent, and an Availability Rate of 95 percent. Although the collection has been reduced by 20 percent, the Performance Rate has climbed from a dismal 45 percent to a sterling 85 percent. Though the libary has shrunk in size, everyone miraculously perceives that it has grown enormously, because suddenly, for the first time, they find books when they want them. Per capita use rates will probably double, while collection maintenance costs plummet.

And the new building that was needed right away will never be needed, because the *number* of volumes required to maintain any specified Performance Rate will remain constant (assuming enrollment does) as the years go by. While the titles held by the library will change from year to year, as patron demand shifts from one book to another, the total number of volumes remains constant. The intake rate of new volumes may be any figure you like (or can afford), because the outflow rate will exactly equal it, if you are firm in your resolve *not* to attempt minor improvements in your Holdings Rate by vastly expanding the number of different books in your collection.

The Alexandrians will be tragically depressed by all this and will curse you both loud and deep for your rampant philistinism. But even they will make the astounding discovery that the books they actually want to read are, as if by magic, suddenly available when they wish to read them. As the opportunities multiply for them actually to read the books they have always wanted to read but never could because the library was so big, their lifelong frustrations with the library will diminish, and eventually they may forget what a wicked trick you played on them.

As for that 11 percent deficiency in your Holdings Rate, much of that can be made up, if you wish, by overhauling your acquisitions and processing operations, so all new English-language imprints will reach your library on or around publication date and be available for circulation a day or so after you receive them. [7] Demand for books is at its peak when they are new. Yet, academic libraries are notorious for average delays of a year or longer in making them available. Eliminating that delay will more than offset the 1 percent Holdings Rate drop that resulted from the removal of 300,000 unused books.

Much of the remaining deficiency in your effective Holdings Rate can be compensated for by participation in an efficient interloan network. Such networks are developing rapidly around the nation, exhibiting Performance Rates in the range of 80 percent, with average delivery times of five days or less.

By these two measures your effective Holdings Rate can be brought at least to 95 percent, and your Performance Rate to a spectacular 90 percent. All of this will cost you substantially less than you would spend to achieve a 45 percent Performance Rate going the traditional exponential growth route. Collection maintenance costs do not usually show up in the library budget, but the university pays for them all the same. They consist of such things as lighting, heating, cooling, janitorial service, and the capital and depreciation costs of real estate. Assuming standard stack capacity of fifteen volumes per square foot, average annual maintenance costs are about twenty cents per volume. Total maintenance costs, of course, grow exponentially so long as the collection does. A million-volume library today has annual collection maintenance costs of $200,000. If the collection doubles every fifteen years, those costs will climb, in forty-five years, to $1,600,000 *per year*.

With what you save in maintenance costs by creating a no-growth collection, you can easily afford a full-scale, rapid-delivery interloan service, to keep your effective Holdings Rate even higher than it was with an exponentially growing collection. With a portion of the savings left over, you can even buy a Gutenberg Bible every year or a Shakespeare First Folio if there are no sellers of the Bible that year. That should convince the Alexandrians that you are not a Philistine after all, but a person of discriminating judgment who prefers to spend his money on things of permanent value—things you just can't get from anybody on interloan.

What to do with the 300,000 volumes you discarded and the 50,000 per year you will discard hereafter? National storage centers are the obvious answer, since, by eliminating multiple copies of discards that will flow in from many libraries, they can cut aggregate storage space requirements by 90 percent or more.

Let us speculate in very general terms on a possible configuration of a system of storage centers and the effect it might have on the space problem nationwide.

Imagine the existence of three storage libraries, each holding books falling into the humanities, the sciences, or the social sciences, and strategically located near major population centers. Imagine further that every academic library in the nation will be distributing to these storage centers two sorts of books: first, those now in their collections that meet the Trueswell criterion for withdrawal, and, later, those that will meet the criterion as the years advance.

What size storage libraries will meet these conditions?

The aggregate content of American academic libraries is presently about 440 million volumes. Assume that a nationwide application of the Trueswell criterion results in the removal of 30 percent of them to storage and that, for ease of illustration, they distribute evenly over the three divisions. We thus have 130 million volumes headed for storage, or 43 million to each of the three storage libraries.

Must each therefore be even bigger than the Library of Congress to accommodate all those books?

Indeed not, for it appears that for each title coming into storage, there will be approximately fifty multiple copies. That estimate arises from the following data: The *National Union Catalog* currently records some 400,000 additional titles each year, while academic libraries acquire some 20 million additional volumes of books. On that basis, which is admittedly rough but adequate for our present speculations, the ratio of titles to copies is 1 to 50.

To be on the conservative side and to broaden geographical distribution of the storage libraries, assume now a complete duplication of the three-library system. Two copies of each title withdrawn from campus libraries will be preserved, and storage libraries will be sited in six locations around the country. The ratio of copies retained to those withdrawn is thus 2 to 50, or 4 percent of all volumes flowing towards the six storage libraries. Thus, initial collection size of each storage library comes to 860,000 volumes.

Our aggregate picture now takes this shape: campus collections reduced by 130 million volumes, and new storage libraries created holding 5 million volumes, for a net gain nationwide in shelving capacity of 125 million volumes.

How much new building space was required to achieve this gain? Assuming eighteen volumes per square foot to be the load ratio in the new storage libraries, 278,000 square feet of new stack area will be required, at a construction cost of 5.6 million dollars.[8]

There will be other costs, of course, and I will touch on them shortly, but ponder for a moment that for 5.6 million dollars in construction you have in effect created space for another 125 million books. To accomplish the same result by constructing new library space on campus would cost about forty times as much, or 250 million dollars.

In each year after the storage libraries are formed, if the Trueswell criterion for creating no-growth libraries is followed nationwide, as many volumes will be removed to storage as are acquired in the course of the year. At present levels (excluding journals), that comes to 20 million volumes being withdrawn each year, of which only 4 percent will actually go into storage, assuming two copies of each title are retained. So each of the six storage libraries will add 133,000 volumes per year, for an aggregate new storage area requirement of about 45,000 square feet per year. Compare that with the 1.3 million square feet of aggregate new construction that would otherwise be required on campuses around the nation, and you will have a good notion of the scale of the economies involved.

To the advanced scholar who maintains that his research depends vitally on access to the sort of book that gets consulted only once in a century, these storage libraries should prove a godsend. For that is the sort of book they will specialize in, and he will find them all under one roof, whereas now he must travel throughout the nation to find only a fraction of what these extraordinary libraries will hold.

Should such a storage system or anything like it ever become reality, the principal cost would arise in the process of identifying books for storage and making the necessary record changes. Using the Trueswell criterion of last recorded circulation date, the cost of identifying titles for storage would be quite low, on the order of ten cents a volume if done by hand and less if done by computer.

But the costs of manually changing catalog and shelf list records to reflect a shift to storage pose a serious obstacle to the whole storage concept. Ralph Ellsworth has estimated them to be in the range of one dollar per book (in 1975 dollars), and that sounds about right.

Here is where I see a role for the computer which will be of vastly greater consequence than anything that has yet been done with it in libraries. Once library catalogs are computerized—and that prospect lies in the very near future—then the cost of changing location records for a book sent to storage should approximate that of handling a loan transaction by computer.

With computerized catalogs and circulation systems, the cost of identifying books for storage and changing their records will be about what it now costs just to keep them in the library for one year. Costs to ship the books to a remote storage library would be substantial, except that 96 percent of the withdrawals need never go there. They can instead go directly to the nearest pulping plant.

"Unto the place from whence the rivers come, thither they return again." That is why, according to Ecclesiastes, the sea is never full. And that is why, once your library has reached a certain size, it need never be full again. How large should that library be? Large enough to satisfy a Performance Rate that is perhaps double what it is now, but always less than 100 percent, which nobody can afford.

When that size is reached, based on your own judgment of what is a satisfactory performance rate, you have a no-growth collection and the means for keeping it so. Your head and your bookstacks are out of the clouds, and your feet have reached the ground. And after 2,300 years you are finally ready to bid a long farewell to Alexandria.

Notes

1. Since my purpose in this sketch is not to debate historical issues, I have generally followed the position of Edward Alexander Parsons' definitive history, *The Alexandrian Library* (New York: American Elsevier, 1967).
2. The Philosophical and Scientific schools may mention, *sotto voce*, the appropriateness of superficial weeding. But nothing of consequence ever came of it. Weeding at significant levels occurs only through theft, which unfortunately removes precisely, and only, those volumes that should not be weeded.
3. I use the term in its extended sense, for convenience, to cover anything a library may supply: books, journals, cassettes, etc.
4. The principal study is R. W. Trueswell, *Analysis of Library User Circulation Requirements, Final Report* (January 1968), N.S.F. Grant GNO 435.
5. While this extreme relationship was observed in at least one collection sampled by Trueswell, he believes that to be at the far end of the range. A conservative estimate, based on his later investigations, is that 60 percent of a collection will account for 99 percent of the recorded use. For the remainder of the argument in this paper, I have based all calculations on an extremely conservative estimate, namely, that 70 percent of a collection will account for 99 percent of recorded use. On that basis, *any* actual library should meet or exceed the expectations raised in my mathematical illustrations.
6. Michael K. Buckland, "An Operations Research Study of a Variable Loan and Duplication Policy at the University of Lancaster," in *Operations Research*, Don R. Swanson and Abraham Bookstein, eds., (Chicago: University of Chicago Press, 1972), pp. 97-106.
7. An economical method for accomplishing this, tested and proved in some thirty college and university libraries to date, is described in my paper "In Hot Pursuit of FASTCAT," *Library Journal* (September 1, 1972): 2693-2695.
8. A conservative estimate, since storage densities could be made much higher than eighteen volumes per square foot and construction costs of an all-stack utility structure, on cheap land, could run well below the $20 per square foot I have used in this calculation. Note that normal shelving density for on-campus libraries is fifteen volumes per square foot, and construction costs at least $30 per square foot.

Touching Bottom In

ACM Conference On
Space, Growth, & Performance Problems
of Academic Libraries

Chicago, April 17-18, 1975
Conrad Hilton Hotel

The Bottomless Pit

PROGRAM
Sessions will convene at The Summit

THURSDAY, APRIL 17

8:30   Coffee and Final Registration
(Lower Summit   use Tower Elevator)

9:45   Welcoming Remarks   Dan Martin,
President of The Associated Colleges of the Midwest

9:50   National Survey and Analysis of the Space
Problem   Claudia Schorrig

10:25   Academic Library Buildings ~ The Next
Ten Years   Ellsworth Mason

11:15   Limiting College Library Growth : Bane
or Boon?   Evan Farber

12:00   Lunch

1:30   Regionalization of University Library Services
Richard Dougherty

2:10   Acquisitions, Growth, and Performance Control
Through Systems Analysis
Michael Buckland and Anthony Hindle

3:10   Growth and Performance Problems of Public
Libraries   Marvin Scilken

3:50   Microtechnology and the Space Problem:
A New Appraisal
Carl Spaulding

Friday, April 18

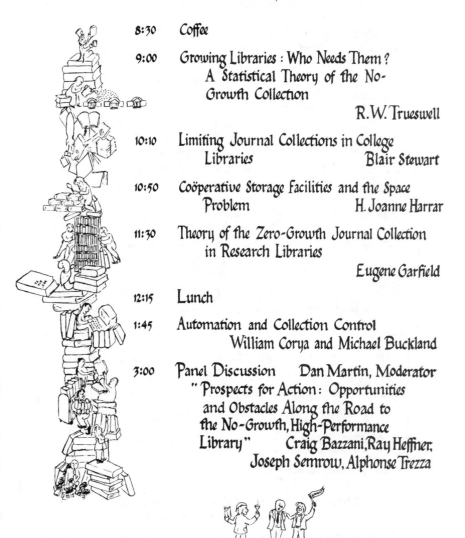

8:30   Coffee

9:00   Growing Libraries : Who Needs Them ?
A Statistical Theory of the No-
Growth Collection
R.W. Trueswell

10:10   Limiting Journal Collections in College
Libraries   Blair Stewart

10:50   Coöperative Storage Facilities and the Space
Problem   H. Joanne Harrar

11:30   Theory of the Zero-Growth Journal Collection
in Research Libraries
Eugene Garfield

12:15   Lunch

1:45   Automation and Collection Control
William Corya and Michael Buckland

3:00   Panel Discussion   Dan Martin, Moderator
" Prospects for Action : Opportunities
and Obstacles Along the Road to
the No-Growth, High-Performance
Library "   Craig Bazzani, Ray Heffner,
Joseph Semrow, Alphonse Trezza

THE SPEAKERS

Michael Buckland, Assistant Director for Technical Services, Purdue University Libraries (formerly head of the operations research team, University of Lancaster Library, England)

William Corya, Head, Systems Unit, Purdue University Libraries

Richard Dougherty, University Librarian, University of California — Berkeley

Evan Farber, Librarian of Earlham College

Eugene Garfield, President, Institute for Scientific Information (publishers of *Science Citation Index*)

H. Joanne Harrar, Associate Director, University of Georgia Libraries

Anthony Hindle, Research Director, Unit for Operational Research in Health Services, University of Lancaster, England

Ellsworth Mason, Director of Libraries, University of Colorado, Boulder

Claudia Schorrig, Assistant Director of Libraries, Florida Atlantic University

Marvin Scilken, Director, Orange (N.J.) Public Library and publisher of *The U·N·A·B·A·S·H·E·D Librarian*

Carl Spaulding, Program Officer, Council on Library Resources

Blair Stewart, Research Director, ACM Periodical Bank and President Emeritus of The Associated Colleges of the Midwest

R.W. Trueswell, Head, Department of Industrial Engineering and Operations Research, University of Massachusetts, and author of the pioneering series of statistical studies of library circulation and inventory phenomena

THE PANELISTS

Craig Bazzani, Budget Analyst, Illinois Bureau of the Budget

Ray Heffner, Professor of English, University of Iowa

Dan Martin, President, The Associated Colleges of the Midwest

Joseph Semrow, Executive Director, North Central Association of Colleges and Schools

Alphonse Trezza, Executive Director, National Commission on Libraries and Information Science

Sponsored by The Associated Colleges of the Midwest
60 West Walton St., Chicago, Illinois 60610

Program chairman Daniel Gore, Library Director, Macalester College